Miller's
GERMAN
Cookbook

By FULTON MILLER

Illustrations by MIKE NELSON

A Nitty Gritty Book*
Published by
Nitty Gritty Productions
P.O. Box 5457
Concord, California 94524

*Nitty Gritty Books - Trademark
Owned by Nitty Gritty Productions
Concord, California

ISBN 0-911954-22-8
Library of Congress Catalog Card Number: 73-151196

TABLE OF CONTENTS

INTRODUCTION

Miller's German Cookbook was originally published in Germany where it was widely acclaimed by Americans traveling and living there.

The Editors have shown all of the recipe titles in both English and German so that the reader will become familiar with the German words. Not only does this help lend authenticity to the recipes, but the reader will find the knowledge of the German words helpful if he ever has occasion to order from a German menu.

Guten Appetit!

FROM 6:00 TO 6:00

Frühstück — Breakfast

The traditional German breakfast is two fresh rolls with butter and jam and a pot of strong coffee. Many Germans eat a boiled egg, cold cuts or cheese. It is not unusual to have a slice of cake or Torte, the German equivalent of pie, and a cup of coffee.

Brotzeit — Mid-morning snack

About ten in the morning a sandwich or roll with ham, cheese or liverwurst and a cup of coffee helps to tide off the hunger pains until lunch. And often a bottle of beer is not at all out of place.

Mittagessen — Lunch

Germans usually eat their big meal at noon. This is the full bit with soup, but seldom a dessert.

Kaffee — Coffee

This is not just coffee. It's coffee with cake at 3:00 or 4:00 in the afternoon.

Abendessen — Dinner

Here we will have to differentiate as there are two schools of thought. One favors a light evening meal of cold cuts, salads or a soup. The other, and I belong to this group, is for the full dinner.

A FARM HIGH
ON THE STEEP
HILLSIDE

vom Rind

Beef

Recipes to serve six

ZWIEBELFLEISCH

Zwiebelfleisch is a dish that comes from Southern Germany and the German part of Switzerland. In fact, Swiss steak is the American derivation of Zwiebelfleisch except for the fact that in Switzerland this is a gourmet's dish -- not a way to tenderize a piece of shoe leather so the family can eat it.

Typical Menu: Suppe -- Soup
Zwiebelfleisch -- Filet steak in rich gravy
Kartoffelpuree -- Mashed potatoes
Grüner Salat -- Green Salad

6 filet steaks, each about 3/4 lb.
1 medium onion
4 tablespoons lard, no substitutes
salt
pepper
flour

Pound each steak ten to fifteen times on each side with a tenderizing hammer or the edge of a saucer. Salt and pepper both sides. Thickly dust one side of the steaks with flour. Cut onion lengthwise in wedges about 1/8 inch thick. Melt lard in pan and place steaks, floured side up, in hot lard. Distribute onion wedges on top of steaks. Brown well. Turn steaks and again brown well. Pour boiling water in pan to just barely cover steaks, cover and simmer slowly for 30 minutes, adding boiling water as necessary to maintain level. Salt and pepper gravy to taste. Serve direct from pan or in a preheated serving dish together with gravy.

SAUERBRATEN

This is a wonderful dish for leftovers. Even if you've made too much, there still won't be any leftover, and the next day you can eat those other leftovers you've had in the refrigerator.

Typical Menu: Backerbsensuppe — "Pea" soup, see pg. 104
Sauerbraten — Marinated pot roast
Kartoffelknödel — See pg. 118. Mashed potatoes, noodles, or potato pancakes also go well with Sauerbraten.

Ingredients For Marinating:
3-1/2 lbs. beef, chuck roast or rump roast
1 cup vinegar
1 cup water
1 small onion
1 carrot
2 sprigs celery leaves

1-1/2 level teaspoons salt
4 cloves
1 large bay leaf
5 whole peppercorns
4 juniper berries

8

Ingredients For Cooking:
1 marrow bone
2 rounded tablespoons lard
2 rounded tablespoons flour
2 small tomatoes
1 pint soup stock
1/2 pint heavy sour cream
salt & pepper to taste

Marinating: Cut the onion in wedges and separate. Cut the carrot in slices about 1/8 inch thick. Put all the ingredients, except the beef, for marinating in an enamel pot. Bring to a low simmer. Cover. Simmer for 15 minutes. Let cool. Wash the beef and place in a glass or plastic container. Pour the marinade over the beef making sure that it is completely covered. If there is not enough marinade to cover beef add boiling water. Cover. Let marinate 3 days unrefrigerated or refrigerated 5 days. Turn beef in marinade once every day.

Cooking: Remove beef from marinade and dry. Retain marinade. Melt lard in frying pan and brown beef and the marrow bone well on all sides. Cut tomatoes in thin wedges and add to pot, mashing them in the hot fat from the frying pan. As soon as tomatoes are soft add vegetables from marinade to pot. Add 1 cup of the marinade, cover and simmer slowly for 1 hour, adding marinade as necessary so that there is always a little water in the pot to keep from burning.

Remove beef and keep warm. Add flour to the melted fat in the pot and stir in. Add soup stock and stir well with a fork to dissolve the crust on the bottom of the pan. Simmer 10 minutes. Stir in sour cream. Again bring to simmer. Salt and pepper to taste. Strain gravy and serve.

TELLERFLEISCH ODER SIEDFLEISCH
(Trencher Meat or Boiled Meat)

This dish has not changed since the middle ages. It is properly and, in Germany, still often, served on a trencher, a wooden plate either round or oval, deeper than a dinner plate, but not as deep as a soup bowl. As the scarred wooden plate is set before you it doesn't take too much imagination to hear a knight in armor clank by on his war horse outside or to see a rotund and red faced friar sit in the corner and mop his brow as he complains of the heat and dust on the road from the abbey.

Typical Menu: Tellerfleisch — Boiled beef
                  Schwarzbrot — Black bread
                  Bier — Beer

2-1/2 lbs. of beef or oxen meat in one piece. This should be about 1-1/2 inches thick and 6 inches wide. This can be cut from the breast or ribs.
2 or 3 marrow bones

1 carrot

1 medium onion

1 bunch of parsley

1 small leek

1 piece of celery as big as your finger

salt

horseradish

Put the meat in a soup pot. Cover with water and bring to a slow boil. Boil for 15 minutes. Skim off scum that forms. Add marrow bones. Cut carrot in half lengthwise, cut roots from onion. Wash and peel onion and retain brown skin. Clean leek and cut in half lengthwise. Add carrot, whole onion, onion skin, leek, celery, 1/2 of a bunch of parsley, and salt to meat. Simmer slowly, covered, for 1-3/4 hours or until meat is tender.

Remove meat from pot and slice crosswise in thin slices. Strain broth from pot. Put meat on plates and pour 1/4 cup of broth over meat. Garnish with parsley and a spoonful of horseradish.

THE ALPS

SUMMIT OF
ZUGSPITZE

KALBSSCHNITZEL NATUR MIT CHAMPIGNONS UND RAHMSOSSE

This is the first of three recipes for Kalbsschnitzel or veal cutlets and the most subtle. With a chilled bottle of Mosel wine it will be a dinner that will be remembered by your guests.

Typical Menu: Einlaufsuppe — Egg drop soup, see pg. 107

Kalbsschnitzel natur mit Champignons and Rahmsosse — Veal cutlet au naturel, with mushrooms and cream sauce.

Rosenkohl — Brussels sprouts

Reis — Rice

Moselwein — Mosel (white) wine

6 veal cutlets, each a little less than 1/2 lb.
1 lb. fresh button mushrooms simmered in butter
lard, no substitutes

14

1 rounded teaspoon flour   2 bunches parsley
1/2 pint sour cream   salt
3 lemons   pepper

Preheat oven to 150°. Wash cutlets and dry. Pound cutlets about ten times on each side with a tenderizing hammer or about fifteen to twenty times on each side with the edge of a saucer. Salt, pepper, and squeeze a few drops of lemon juice on both sides.

Melt 1 tablespoon lard in pan and fry Schnitzels until done, adding lard as necessary. As Schnitzels are done, place in oven to keep warm. A little before the last Schnitzels are done add well-drained button mushrooms and flour to pan, stirring flour well into melted lard so that it browns. Remove Schnitzels from pan and place in oven to keep warm. Turn fire very low. Stir sour cream into pan, stirring well to dissolve crust from bottom of pan. Bring to simmer. The sauce will be a very light brown. Place Schnitzels on prewarmed plates garnished with lemon wedges and parsley. Pour sauce with mushrooms over Schnitzels.

PAPRIKA-RAHMSCHNITZEL

The first Kalbsschnitzel recipe was subtle. The second was piquant. The third, and last, is subtle and piquant. Actually, it is a combination of the first two.

Typical Menu: Tomatensuppe — Tomato soup
                       Paprika-Rahmschnitzel — Schnitzel with bell peppers in cream
                           sauce
                       Reis — Rice
                       Rot-oder Weisswein — Red or white wine

Same as for Kalbsschnitzel mit Rahmsosse, see pg. 14
plus
1 medium onion
3 medium green or red bell peppers

Prepare as for Kalbsschnitzel, pg. 14. While the Schnitzels are cooking cut peppers in half and remove stems and seeds. Cut crosswise in thin half-rings. Peel onion, cut in half lengthwise, then into thin slices. Fry pepper half-rings and onion half-rings in a small frying pan until soft. Just after adding the sour cream add fried peppers and onions to sauce. Let simmer 1 minute. Place Schnitzels on prewarmed plates. Pour sauce with mushrooms, peppers, and onions on Schnitzels and garnish with parsley and lemon wedges.

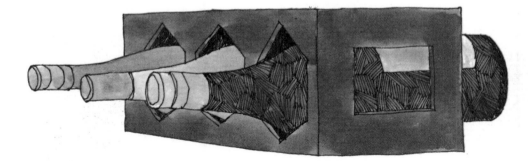

PAPRIKASCHNITZEL

Where the first Schnitzel was subtle this is piquant.

Typical Menu: Tomatensuppe — Tomato soup
Paprikaschnitzel — Schnitzel with bell peppers
Bratkartoffeln — Hash brown potatoes
Endiviensalat — Endive salad
Rotwein — Red wine

6 veal cutlets, each a little less than 1/2 lb.
lard, no substitutes
3 lemons
3 medium green or red peppers
1 medium onion
salt
pepper

Preheat oven to 150°. Wash cutlets and dry. Pound cutlets about ten times on each side with a tenderizing hammer or fifteen to twenty times on each side with the edge of a saucer. Salt, pepper, and squeeze a few drops of lemon juice on both sides.

Cut peppers in half lengthwise. Remove stems and seeds. Wash. Cut peppers crosswise in thin half-ring slices. Peel onion and cut in half lengthwise, cut in thin half-rings. Cut lemons lengthwise, then in thin half-circle slices.

In a large pan melt lard and fry Schnitzels to a golden brown. As they are done place them in the oven to keep warm.

While the Schnitzels are frying, melt some lard in a medium frying pan and fry pepper rings and onion rings until soft. Remove pan from heat and keep warm.

Place Schnitzels on prewarmed plates. Put pepper rings and onions on the Schnitzels alternating with lemon slices. Pour a little of the grease from the pan over the pepper, onions, and lemon slices on the Schnitzels.

WIENER SCHNITZEL

A short lesson on Wiener Schnitzels. They are named after Vienna which, in German, is spelled Wien and pronounced "veen". They don't have a thing to do with weenies.

A Wiener Schnitzel should be:
1. Light as a feather
2. Golden brown
3. Crisp outside
4. Juicy inside
If it's not all four, it's not, definitely not, a Wiener Schnitzel.

Typical Menu: Suppe — Soup
                  Wiener Schnitzel — Breaded veal cutlet Viennese style
                  Kartoffelsalat — Potato salad
                  Überbackener Blumenkohl — Baked cauliflower, see pg. 127

DINKELSBÜHL ESTABLISHED
IN THE 6TH OR 7TH CENTURY

M. NELSON

6 veal cutlets as large as your hand, 3/8 inch thick
2 eggs
3 cups bread crumbs
lard, no substitutes
salt
pepper
2 lemons
3 small firm tomatoes
2 bunches parsley

Preheat oven to 180°. Wash Schnitzels and dry; pound them about ten times on each side with a tenderizing hammer or about fifteen to twenty times on each side with the edge of a saucer. Salt and pepper both sides.

Break eggs in a bowl, salt and pepper, and beat well with a fork. Heat lard in frying pan (with two pans you will be finished sooner). Prewarm 6 plates.

Dip Schnitzel in egg, both sides, then in bread crumbs. It must be completely and quite thickly covered. Fry in frying pan on medium high heat. Do not crowd Schnitzels in the pan. As soon as outside is golden brown reduce heat and continue frying until done through. Repeat the above procedure with the remaining Schnitzels. As the Schnitzels are done, place on a cookie sheet in the prewarmed oven to keep hot until all are done. Place on prewarmed plates, garnish with tomato wedges, parsley, and a lemon wedge. Serve immediately. Let the guests squeeze the lemon juice on the Schnitzels at the table.

Pork cutlets can also be used for Wiener Schnitzels. Some cooks prefer to sprinkle the Schnitzel with lemon juice and then let marinate for 15 minutes before dipping in the beaten egg.

SCHMORBRATEN

You know there really isn't anything better than good beef.

Typical Menu: Einlaufsuppe — Egg drop soup, see pg. 107
Schmorbraten — Pot roast
Kartoffelpüree — Mashed potatoes
Gemischter Salat — Mixed salad

3-1/2 lbs. beef, chuck roast or rump roast
2 rounded tablespoons lard, no substitutes
2 rounded tablespoons flour
1 small onion
1 carrot
2 sprigs parsley
1 sprig celery leaves
1 small leek

2 small tomatoes
1 pint soup stock
1 large bay leaf, optional
salt and pepper

Peel onion, carrot and celery. Cut onion in wedges, carrot, celery, and leek in strips. Slice tomatoes. Rub beef with salt and pepper. Melt lard in pan and brown beef very well on all sides. Add flour and onions, stir in and brown. Mash in tomatoes and add other vegetables. Add soup stock, stirring to dissolve crust in pan. Cover and simmer very slowly until done. Salt and pepper gravy, strain through a sieve and serve.

RINDSROULADE

As usual I was late arriving at the station so I had to run the last fifty meters to the train. Finding my compartment, I said "Guten Tag" to the two other occupants, removed my coat and hat, placed my suitcase on the rack above my seat and settled in my seat. About twenty minutes after we left Köln (Cologne) we stopped at Bonn. It was almost noon, so I went forward to the dining car. The Oberkellner presented me a menu and bowing slightly said "Darf ich die Rindsroulade empfehlen?" ("May I recommend the Rindsroulade?"). "Gut, und bitte einen Rheinwein, nicht zu herb." ("Good, and a bottle of Rhinewine, not too dry, please".)

So, if you happen to be riding on the Bundesbahn, German National Railways, "Darf ich eine Rindsroulade empfehlen?"

Typical Menu: Suppe — Soup. This should be light.
                 Rindsroulade — Filled beef roll
                 Kartoffelpürre — Mashed potatoes

6 round steaks, sliced thin, about 3/16 inch thick. The slices should be about 7
inches wide and 10 to 11 inches long. They will weigh a little less than 1/2 lb.
each.

salt & pepper to taste
12 strips of lean bacon
1 large carrot
1 large dill pickle
German mustard — this is the brown, hot mustard
thread
flour
lard or fat
1 medium onion cut in wedges about 1/8 inch thick
1 level tablespoon flour
5 cups boiling water
1 cup cream, optional

Wash and dry the round steak slices. Salt and pepper lightly on both sides. Spread about 1/2 to 3/4 teaspoon mustard evenly on one side of each Roulade. Cut the bacon in pieces about 1 inch long and place the pieces equally distributed on the Roulades. Cut the carrot and dill pickle in strips about as large as a pencil and as long as the Roulades are wide. Divide the strips among Roulades. Place the carrot and pickle strips on one end of the Roulade and roll the Roulade together like a jelly roll tucking the ends in as you roll. Tie together firmly with thread. Roll Roulade in flour until well coated.

Heat fat in pan. Brown Roulades well on all sides adding fat as necessary. If the pan is not large enough remove Roulades as they become brown until all are browned. Add one tablespoon flour and stir in well. Add onion and brown until glassy. Add remaining Roulades previously removed. Add boiling water slowly, stir well with fork to dissolve crust on bottom of pan and to prevent lumps. Cover pan. Simmer slowly for 1 hour. Remove from stove, let cool and place in refrigerator over night. Before serving, simmer 1/4 hour. Salt and pepper gravy to taste and stir in cream if desired.

MILKMAID –
ON THE HIGH
MEADOWS OF THE
KÖNIGSBERGERALM

STEAK GARNIERT

A good steak medium well or medium rare, to your taste, is the starting point for this recipe rather than the end product. Steak garniert, under various names, is popular from the North Sea to the Alps.

Typical Menu: Suppe — Soup
Steak garniert — "Garnished" Steak
Champignons — Mushrooms
Pommes frites — French fried potatoes
Zigeunersalat — Paprika salad

6 fillet steaks, each about 3/4 lb.
lard, no substitutes
salt
pepper
6 thin slices Canadian bacon or smoked ham
6 thin slices Emmentaler or Cheddar cheese

butter
2 lbs. fresh, cleaned, drained mushrooms
Worcestershire sauce
6 tomato wedges
6 toothpicks

Brown mushrooms in butter in the medium frying pan, salt and keep warm.

Melt lard in large pan. Salt and pepper steaks on both sides. Brown steaks on both sides in hot lard. Cook almost to the desired doneness. On each steak add a dash of Worcestershire sauce, then place a slice of Canadian bacon followed by a slice of cheese then another dash of Worcestershire. Pour mushrooms over steaks. Cover pan. As soon as cheese has melted place a tomato wedge on each steak, secure with a tooth pick and serve.

TATAR

Tatar beefsteak is quite popular for an evening snack or at parties. It is exceptionally good with red wine.

Typical Menu: Tatar — Raw beef, ground
Schwarzbrot — Black bread
Rotwein — Red wine

3 lbs. lean, fresh, tender, red beef
6 eggs
onion
parsley
salad oil
tarragon vinegar
Worcestershire sauce
caraway seeds
horseradish

hot mustard
hot paprika powder
salt
peppercorns

Wash the beef and remove all sinews and fat. Grind. Arrange the beef on each plate to form a nest. Separate yolks from eggs and place a raw egg yolk in each beef nest. Garnish with parsley. Dice the onions and serve onions and other condiments in separate dishes. Let each guest season to his own taste.

LABSKAUS

Labskaus is strictly North German; Bremen, Hamburg, the North Sea coast. Traditionally it is a seaman's dish, and I wonder if this isn't because all of the ingredients could be kept for long periods of time without refrigeration on the old sailing ships.

Typical Menu: Labskaus — Corned beef, potato, beet "one dish"
                       Rote Rüben — Red beets
                       Rollmops — Roll mops, pickled herring
                       Pils — Pilsener Beer

2 one lb. cans corned beef
5 large potatoes
3 large beets
1 large onion
6 medium pickles
6 eggs

12 roll mops, pickled herring
butter or margarine
salt

Peel potatoes and beets. Cook in salted water separately until done. Retain water from beets. Mash potatoes dry (use no butter or milk). Cut beets in thin slices. Mince corned beef. Mash one half of the beet slices and the corned beef together with the potatoes to a uniform consistency. Add beet water to provide coloring until the mass has the consistency of a stiff pudding. Cut onions in thin rings and pickles in fans. Fry eggs in butter. Rewarm the Labskaus. On each plate place a serving of Labskaus, topped with a fried egg and a pickle fan on the side. On a separate plate place the remaining beet slices and roll mops and garnish with onion rings.

ROTHENBURG

vom Schwein

Pork

Recipes to serve six

SCHWEINEFLEISCH MIT SAUERKRAUT

"You know, Herman, it gifs nichts better dann ein goot Schweinefleisch mit sauerkraut." Hearing the conversation of the two taxi drivers leaning on a cab at the taxi stand before the Rathaus made me think of lunch. Actually, practically anything makes me think of lunch, and if not lunch, of breakfast or dinner.

Entering the Hofbrauhaus garden, it was warm and sunny. I found a table that was full and asked the inhabitants (in Bavaria the Bavarians tend to inhabit a table in a beer garden rather than just sit there) to "Ruck a'bisser!" ("Slide over a little") and sat down. In Bavaria you would never dream of sitting down at any empty table. There wouldn't be anyone to talk to and that's no way to enjoy lunch. It's ungemütlich, in fact, in Bavaria, it's damn near antisocial. I didn't need to order a Mass (stein) of beer. That appeared automatically.

Looking through the Speisekarte (menu) I ordered a Schweinefleisch mit Sauerkraut and another Mass. In Bavaria menus are long and, due to the proximity to the Alps, beer evaporates repidly. Finishing the Schweinefleisch I ordered another Mass and engaged in the discussion, as to whether the Bundeskanzler (Chancellor of Germany) really was a complete idiot, with my neighbor. Three Masses of beer, four pretzels and five hours later we had solved the political future of Germany in general and Bavaria in particular. A newly arriving guest asked for a menu and this made me think of dinner and a Mass of beer. After all, I always drink a beer with dinner.

Typical Menu: Bier — Beer

Schweinefleisch mit Sauerkraut — Pork and sauerkraut

Bier — Beer

Bretzen — Pretzels

Bier — Beer

Bier — Beer

Bier — Beer

2 lbs. fresh sauerkraut from the barrel or 2 one pound cans sauerkraut, 3 if not
tightly packed

1-1/2 tablespoons lard, no substitutes

1 medium onion

2 to 3 lbs. fairly lean pork

18 dried juniper berries

2 level teaspoons salt

1 rounded tablespoon flour

1/4 cup cold water

If you use fresh sauerkraut: Wash and drain it. Melt the lard in a pot. Add sauerkraut and simmer slowly about 5 minutes, turning often with a fork until the kraut has absorbed the melted lard. Add boiling water to cover kraut, cover pot and simmer until tender, adding boiling water as necessary to keep the kraut covered. This will be about 2 hours, depending on the kraut. Proceed as below.

If you use canned sauerkraut: Wash and drain it. Melt the lard in a pot. Add sauerkraut and simmer slowly about 5 minutes, turning often with a fork until the kraut has absorbed the melted lard. Add boiling water to cover kraut. Proceed as below.

Cut the pork in large chunks and salt on all sides. Add pork, the onion, peeled but not cut up, and the juniper berries. Mix pork with kraut until it is covered and simmer slowly, covered, 1 hour or until pork is done. Mix flour with 1/4 cup cold water and stir into kraut. Add salt. Note: Since sauerkrauts vary greatly in salt content, add salt a little at a time to taste. Cook an additional 10 minutes before serving.

SCHWEINEBRATEN (Roast Pork)

Go in any Gasthaus in Southern Germany . . . Schweinebraten! In Bavaria it's the traditional dish, the national dish, the most popular dish, it's, it's . . . it's Schweinebraten!

Typical Menu: Suppe — Soup
                  Schweinebraten -- Roast pork with Kartoffelknödel, page 118
                  Gemischter Salat — Mixed salad
                  Bier — Beer

3 lb. pork roast
1 medium onion
1 tablespoon lard, no substitutes
1 rounded tablespoon flour
1 garlic clove
salt
pepper

For the gravy:
1 tomato
2 rounded tablespoons flour
2 pints boiling water

42

Wash meat. Salt and pepper and rub in. Peel the onion and cut in wedges, lengthwise, about 1/8 inch thick. Put meat, onion, lard and garlic clove in roasting pan. Sprinkle with a rounded tablespoon flour. Put in hot, 475°—500° oven. Roast 20 minutes or until brown. Turn meat once so it browns on all sides. Turn oven down to 350°—400° and roast slowly about 2-1/2 hours or until done. From time to time pour 1/2 cup boiling water over the meat and baste with the melted fat in the pan. Add the tomato to the pan 20 minutes before the pork is done and mash in with a fork.

When the meat is done, remove from the pan and keep warm. Mix 2 rounded tablespoons flour with cold water and add to pan. Stir well. Add 2 pints boiling water. Salt and pepper to taste. Return meat to pan and place in oven for another 15 minutes. The meat can be sliced before returning to the pan or left whole. It all depends on whether you want it crisp or not. Remove from oven, strain gravy and serve hot.

KASSLER RIPPCHEN MIT SAUERKRAUT

A "Kassler und ein Glas Bier" is a German lunch time standby from the finest restaurants to the "Schnellimbisse" (quick lunch counters). That is to say it's the German's "Hamburger n'french fries n'cup-a-coffee."

Typical Menu: Kassler Rippchen mit Sauerkraut — Smoked pork chops with sauerkraut
Salzkartoffeln — Boiled potatoes, optional or
Kartoffelpüree — Mashed potatoes, optional
Bier — Beer   Römer — Caraway rolls

12 smoked pork chops   2 lbs. sauerkraut, see pg. 122   German mustard

Warm sauerkraut, adding a little water to make steam. Steam chops in kraut, covered, 10 to 15 minutes. Serve with the mustard pot within easy reach. In America, if you can't get smoked pork chops, use thick slices of smoked Canadian bacon.

A TOAST AT A
BEER GARDEN

SAUERFLEISCH

Sauerfleisch is a highly spiced dish peculiar to the Allgäu. I have never seen it anywhere else. You will either love it or hate it, no one ever feels neutral.

Typical Menu: Sauerfleisch — Sour spiced pork
Kartoffelpüree — Mashed potatoes
Bier — Beer or Rotwein — Red Wine

3 lbs. fairly lean pork
2 lbs. onions
1 rounded tablespoon finely
    minced carrot
2 quarts water
1/2 cup vinegar
20 dried juniper berries
30 whole dried peppercorns

5 allspice berries
10 cloves
1-1/2 teaspoons whole dried mustard seeds
2 tablespoons whole dried coriander
3 large bay leaves, crushed
6 drops tabasco sauce or
    3 small whole dried chile peppers

1/4 teaspoon ground, not powdered, marjoram
3/4 teaspoon caraway seeds
1/4 teaspoon sugar
1/4 teaspoon cinnamon
2 level teaspoons salt, add more if required before serving.

Cut meat in chunks 1-1/2 to 2 inches square. Cut onions in thin rings. Add all ingredients to large soup pot with cover and cook for 1 to 1-1/2 hours until meat is very tender.

Put generous helpings of mashed potatoes in soup bowls. Place the Sauerfleisch in the soup bowls then ladle onions and soup over the Sauerfleisch and mashed potatoes. Serve with soup spoons.

Incidentally, I should make a comment here. The spices in this dish are not to be removed before serving. It is the kaleidoscope of taste that varies from bite to bite as you bite into a coriander seed, a juniper berry or a caraway seed that makes this dish extraordinary.

PANIERTES KOTELETT

I know you already know how to make breaded pork chops, but no German cook book would be complete without them.

Typical Menu: Paniertes Kotelett — Breaded pork chop
Kartoffelsalat — Potato salad, hot or cold
Grüner Salat — Green salad

6 large T-bone type pork chops	salt
2 or 3 eggs	pepper
2 cups bread crumbs	3 lemons
lard	

Wash chops. Rub in salt and pepper. Sprinkle with a few drops of lemon juice. Let marinate 1/2 hour. Beat eggs. Dip chops in eggs, then in bread crumbs. Coat well with bread crumbs as this gives that delicious crispy outside. Fry in hot lard until brown. Reduce heat and fry until done. Serve with lemon wedges.

SCHWEINSHAXN VOM SPIESS

The aroma of Schweinshaxn on the rotisserie will drive the neighborhood wild. Try this on the evening that the neighbor you don't like is serving her husband cold leftovers after he has been mixing cement for their new patio all day. It even works better if the wind is blowing in their direction.

Typical Menu: Schweinshaxn — Roast pork hocks   Semmeln — Rolls
                      Gemischter Salat — Mixed salad   Bier — Beer

3 pork hocks, not ham—they must be fresh pork, each between 2 and 2-1/2 lbs.
salt; peppercorns, unground

Wash and dry the hocks. With a very sharp pointed knife slit the skin in a crisscross pattern of half inch squares 1/2 inch deep. Rub with salt and freshly ground pepper. Roast on the rotisserie at high heat until very well done. This will take from 2-1/2 to 4 hours depending on the rotisserie and the size of the hocks. If the skin starts to burn move further from heat.

KOTELETT IN ASPIK

Sülze or Aspik is a way of dressing up foods so they have that good old S A for the cold buffet or lunch.

Typical Menu: Kotelett in Aspik — Smoked pork chop in aspic
Kartoffelsalat mit Mayonnaise — Potato salad with mayonnaise
Toastbrot — Toast

6 smoked, cooked pork chops or 6 cooked pork chops or 6 thick slices of cooked
    Canadian bacon
1 quart clear bouillon
clear gelatin; check the package for amount for 1 quart liquid
3 hard-boiled eggs
6 small pickles
6 sprigs tarragon
2 medium tomatoes
1 bunch parsley

1/4 cup vinegar
butter
salt
pepper
mayonnaise

Heat the bouillon. Add the vinegar. Add the gelatin according to the instructions on the package. Pour about 1/8 inch aspic, liquid but not hot, into very lightly buttered individual forms, a little larger than the pork chops, or into a flat casserole. Place in refrigerator to set.

When aspic is firm, place a twig of tarragon, then an egg slice, then a pork chop on top in each mold. Garnish with remaining egg slices, pickle slices and tomato slices around the chop. Pour in additional aspic, cool not hot, carefully. Jar the mold so that bubbles are not entrapped. Chill until set. Dip forms in hot water, invert. Garnish with parsley and mayonnaise.

IN THE VINEYARDS
ABOVE THE RHINE

Verſchiedenes

Various meat dishes

Recipes to serve six

SCHINKENNUDELN

Schinkennudeln is a plain and tasty dish. It's a good way to use up leftover ham. Actually, who really ever has any "leftover" ham? Maybe after a big party or family reunion you might have two pounds of leftover ham, but then again that probably wouldn't be the case either. After a family reunion when my relatives have left, there isn't any leftover ham, or leftover anything else for that matter. They eat everything. The last time my brother-in-law was here my daughter had been cutting out pictures of Ritz crackers from the carton and before I noticed what was happening he had almost choked to death on one. Fortunately he found a case of beer to wash the bad taste out of his mouth.

So I guess it's better to forget what I started to say about leftovers and just go ahead and buy the ham.

Typical Menu: Schinkennudeln — Ham and noodles
                 Grüner Salat — Green salad

2 lbs. boiled ham

54

1 lb. wide egg noodles
1 level tablespoon salt
2 teaspoons oil
1 medium onion
2 rounded tablespoons lard
3 tablespoons minced chives
pepper

Bring water to a rolling boil in a large pot. Add salt and noodles and add oil to prevent foaming over. Cook noodles until tender, about 15 minutes, stirring occasionally with a wooden spoon to prevent sticking to bottom of the pot. When done, quench with cold water and drain.

Dice ham and onion. Melt lard in a frying pan. Brown ham and onions lightly. Add noodles and mix together. Cook together, stirring and turning noodles until ham and noodles are well mixed and hot through. Transfer to a serving dish. Sprinkle with minced chives, then pepper and serve.

KÖNIGSBERGER KLOPSE

The evening was for crystal chandeliers, crystal, fine china, candlelight, a light white wine, something pleasing for highly refined tastes.

Typical Menu: Suppe — Soup. This should be light.
Königsberger Klopse — Delicate croquettes in sauce
Kartoffelpüree — Mashed potatoes
Spargel — Asparagus
Nachtisch — Dessert

For the Klopse:
1-3/4 lbs. ground meat, mixture of beef and pork
9 slices white bread, stale, with crusts removed
2 cups, loosely filled, cooked, grated potatoes
5 anchovy fillets
2 eggs

1 level tablespoon flour
3/8 level teaspoon salt
2 tablespoons capers
a dash of pepper

For the sauce:

3 rounded tablespoons butter   1-1/2 teaspoons lemon juice
2 rounded tablespoons flour   1/2 rounded teaspoon salt
3 tablespoons capers   pepper
4 cups soup stock

Soak bread in water about 2 minutes, then squeeze out. Mince anchovies as fine as possible. Blend meat, bread, potatoes, minced anchovies, eggs, flour, salt, pepper, and capers together well. Form eighteen balls about the size of small eggs (three per person). Roll balls in flour and drop in a large deep pot of medium boiling salted water for 12 minutes. Remove and keep warm.

Melt butter in a large pot with cover. Add flour and blend well with fork. Do not brown. Add capers, lemon juice, salt and pepper. Add boiling soup stock. Stir well with a fork or egg whisk to prevent lumps. Simmer slowly, covered, for 15 minutes, stirring frequently to prevent burning. Add Klopse to sauce and simmer for 5 minutes. Serve.

HAMMELFLEISCH MIT GRÜNEN BOHNEN or GRÜNE BOHNEN-EINTOPF

Lamb and green bean pot. Tastes good. Serve as a one dish meal.

2 to 2-1/2 lbs. tender lamb
6 strips bacon
lard
1 medium onion
3 lbs. green snap beans or
      3 No. 2 cans cut string beans

2 lbs. potatoes
4 tablespoons fresh savory, chopped
1 garlic clove
salt
pepper

Wash meat and cut in 1 inch cubes. Cut bacon crosswise in strips 1 inch long. Dice onion. Fry onion and bacon with garlic clove until brown. Remove from pot. Discard garlic and fry lamb cubes until brown on all sides, adding a little lard if necessary. Remove from fire. Peel potatoes and cut in large chunks. Clean beans and cut in 1-1/2 inch lengths. Add all ingredients to pot and add 1-1/2 pints cold water. Bring to boil. Cover. Simmer slowly 1 to 1-1/2 hours. Salt and pepper to taste.

FLEISCHPFLANZL

I suppose every country in the world has its own version of the meat ball or hamburger, and not only its own version, but a hundred variations of the same. The Fleischpflanzl is one of the German versions. Each cook has his own recipe, this is mine.

Typical Menu: Fleischpflanzl — A kind of hamburger
Kartoffelsalat — Potato salad, hot or cold
Grüner Salat — Green salad or Krautsalat — Sauerkraut salad, see pg. 139
Schwarzbrot — Black bread

1 cup diced onion
1/3 cup finely chopped parsley
1-3/4 lbs. ground meat (1/2 beef, 1/2 pork)
lard
9 slices stale white bread with the crusts removed

1-1/2 level teaspoon salt
1/8 teaspoon pepper
3 small or 2 large eggs
3 rounded teaspoons flour

In a small frying pan fry the diced onions and the finely chopped parsley together until the onions are glassy. Dip the bread slices in a bowl of water about 30 seconds, then squeeze out well.

In a mixing bowl add hamburger, fried onions and parsley, the squeezed out bread, salt, pepper, and the eggs. Mix together well until you can't see meat or bread, just a uniform mixture. Sprinkle the flour over the mixture and mix in well. Heat lard in large frying pan. With wet hands form mixture in balls about the size of an egg. Makes eighteen. Press flat in patties a little thicker than a quarter of an inch. Fry in hot lard until both sides are crisp, then turn heat down and fry slowly for about 10 to 15 minutes until done through.

A Fleischpflanzl should be crisp on the outside and juicy on the inside. If the frying pan is not large enough to fry the Fleischpflanzls all at one time remove the finished Pflanzls from the pan and keep warm in a 180° oven, uncovered, until all are done. Serve three per person.

SPECKHACKBRATEN

Being a long time friend of meat loaf I just couldn't leave this recipe out.

Typical Menu: Suppe — Soup
                      Speckhackbraten — Meat loaf (with bacon)
                      Kartoffelpüree — Mashed potatoes
                      Grüner Salat — Green salad
                      Semmeln — Rolls

2 lbs. hamburger (1-1/2 lbs. beef, 1/2 lb. pork)
10 strips of bacon
lard
10 slices stale white bread with the crusts removed
1 cup finely diced onions
2 tablespoons finely chopped parsley
1/2 small carrot
2 rounded tablespoons flour

2 eggs
2 level teaspoons salt
1/8 teaspoon freshly ground pepper

For the gravy:	4 cups soup stock
1 medium onion	lard
2 rounded tablespoons flour	salt
1 medium tomato	pepper

In a small frying pan saute the diced onions and the finely chopped parsley together until the onions are glassy. Dip the bread slices in a bowl of water about 30 seconds, then squeeze out well. Cut seven of the strips of bacon in 1 inch lengths. Mince the piece of carrot.

In a mixing bowl add hamburger, fried onions and parsley, the 1 inch pieces of bacon, carrot, the squeezed-out bread, flour, eggs, salt and pepper. Mix together well until you can't see meat or bread, just a uniform mixture. Grease a roasting pan (not glass) well. Form mixture in a loaf. Cut the remaining 3 slices of bacon in half and place crosswise on the loaf and press firmly in place. Bake in a 375° oven until done, about 1 hour.

Turn off oven and leave door open. Remove meat loaf from oven. Carefully remove meat loaf from pan with an egg turner and place on a serving platter. Place serving platter in oven to keep warm.

Put pan on top of stove and turn on heat. There should be about 2 to 3 tablespoons of melted fat in the pan. If not, add lard. Finely mince onion and brown until light brown. Add flour, stirring well with a fork. Brown well. Slice tomato and add to onions and flour. Mash in with a fork. Cook another 2 to 3 minutes. Add boiling soup stock slowly, stir well with a fork to dissolve crust on bottom of pan and to prevent lumps. Simmer slowly 5 minutes. Strain through a fine sieve or dish towel. Serve on or with the meat loaf.

BALTIC SEA BEACH
NEAR KIEL

TIROLER GERÖSTEL

If you really want to serve this right, buy a record of zither music by Anton Karas, put some beer in the ice box to cool, and slip into a low cut dirndl.

Typical Menu: Tiroler Geröstel — Tyrolean hash
Grüner Salat — Green salad
Schwarzbrot — Black bread   Bier — Beer

1 lb. leftover beef, either cooked
 or roast, preferably roast
4 eggs, optional
2 medium onions

3-1/2 lbs. potatoes, preferably new potatoes
1/3 cup loosely packed, chopped parsley
lard, no substitutes
salt & pepper

Cook peeled potatoes in salted water until barely tender; drain and set aside. Dice peeled onions and the meat; brown them lightly in hot lard in frying pan. Add 1/8 inch potato slices, mix well together and brown. Add salt and pepper, and eggs. When eggs are set, sprinkle with chopped parsley and serve.

66

PICHELSTEINER

Pichelsteiner is one of the most favorite "Eintopfs", one pot dinners, in the Fatherland. This is a man's dish for healthy appetites after an afternoon of wood-chopping.

Typical Menu: Pichelsteiner — Beef, veal, lamb, and pork stew
Schwarzbrot — Black bread, in thick slices
Butter — Butter   Bier — Beer

1/2 lb. lean stew beef
1/2 lb. lean veal
1/2 lb. lean lamb
1/2 lb. lean pork
1/2 of a small head of white cabbage
4 lbs. potatoes
1/2 lb. carrots
1 medium onion

1 medium leek
1 handful celery leaves
1 bunch parsley
lard
1 quart soup stock
salt
freshly ground black pepper, no substitute

Wash meats and cut in 3/4 inch cubes. Salt and pepper and mix together. Cut stem from cabbage and separate leaves. Cut each leaf in half along the vein. Peel potatoes and cut in slices, crosswise, about 1/4 inch thick. Clean carrots and cut in slices, crosswise, about 1/16 inch thick. Peel onion and cut in wedges lengthwise, about 1/8 inch thick. Separate the layers of onion. Clean leek, cut in half lengthwise, then crosswise in slices about 1/8 inch thick. Chop celery leaves rather rough. Divide meat into three piles and vegetables into three piles.

Grease bottom of a large stew pot with lard. Line pot with 1/3 of the cabbage leaves, then a layer of one third of the meat and vegetables. Salt and grind pepper over this layer. Repeat for the next two layers. That is to say: Cabbage leaves, meat and vegetables, salt and pepper. Add the cold soup stock. Place on stove, cover, bring to a slow boil and cook 1 to 1-1/4 hours or until beef is tender. Important: Do not stir or you will end up with a mush. Pour in soup tureen to serve, or serve directly from the pot.

LINSENEINTOPF (MIT WIENERWÜRSTCHEN)

Genesis 25:

29 And Jacob sod pottage: and Esau came from the field, and he was faint:

30 And Esau said to Jacob, Feed me, I pray thee, with that same red pottage: for I am faint: . . .

34 Then Jacob gave Esau bread and pottage of lentiles: and he did eat and drink, and rose up, and went his way: . . .

Typical Menu: Linseneintopf (mit Wienerwürstchen) — Lentil pot, wienerwursts
Schwarzbrot — Black bread

1-1/2 lbs. (4 measuring cups) dried lentils
1-1/4 tablespoons vinegar
2-1/2 level teaspoons salt
1 medium onion
1 medium carrot
10 strips bacon

69

1/8 teaspoon pepper
12 wienerwursts, optional

Soak the lentils overnight. Drain and wash in a sieve. Place in a large soup pot, cover with cold water and bring to a boil. Cover. Simmer slowly for 1 to 2 hours. Add boiling water if necessary so lentils remain covered.

Dice onion and carrot. Cut bacon in 1 inch lengths and fry crisp. Remove bacon and brown onions. Add fried bacon, fat from pan, onions, carrot, salt, pepper, and vinegar to the simmering lentils and continue cooking for another hour. If desired add wienerwursts 15 minutes before cooking is complete. Serve hot.

KRAUTWICKEL

Krautwickel, stuffed cabbage leaves, is another popular dish in Bavaria. As you enter an old Gasthaus about twelve-thirty in the afternoon and take a seat in one of the booths along the dark paneled walls you will see a hurried business-man, a little old lady or two, and several robust Bavarians between seventeen and seventy making enormous portions of delicious Krautwickel disappear. As the Kellnerin, waitress, comes to your table you order a beer and a Krautwickel. "Leider, Krautwickel ist aus." ("Sorry, we are out of Krautwickel.") So, reluctantly you pick up the menu and decide to come earlier tomorrow, before the Krautwickel is "aus".

Typical Menu: Krautwickel — Stuffed cabbage leaves
                    Kartoffelpüree — Mashed potatoes
                    Bier — Beer

2 lbs. ground meat
1 large head of white cabbage, about 10 inches in diameter

2 eggs
1 medium onion
1 rounded teaspoon finely chopped parsley
1 level teaspoon ground, not powdered, marjoram
2 level teaspoons caraway seeds
1-1/2 level teaspoons salt
pepper
lard
2 to 3 cups soup stock
thread

Wash cabbage and cut out center stem. Put about 2 inches of water in a cooking pot and some salt. Put cabbage head upright in water, cover and steam. As the outer leaves become tender, remove cabbage from pot and peel off the tender leaves. Set leaves aside to drain.

Return cabbage to pot and repeat until all the leaves are removed. Make six piles of two to three of the large outside cabbage leaves. Finely dice the remaining smaller cabbage leaves from the heart. This should give about two cups. Finely dice the onion. Add the diced cabbage leaves, onion, parsley, marjoram, caraway, salt, some pepper and the eggs to the ground meat and mix well. Divide the meat mixture into six equal portions. Form each of the portions in the shape of a small meat loaf and wrap in the large cabbage leaves. Make sure that the meat is completely wrapped with two or three layers of cabbage leaves. Tie well with thread.

Melt lard in frying pan and brown, but do not burn, the Krautwickel on all sides. Pour fat from frying pan into a roasting pan, add Krautwickel and boiling soup stock. Cover. Place pan across two burners of the stove and simmer slowly for 1 to 1-1/2 hours.

This can also be done in the oven, however if cooked in the oven the Krautwickel must be basted from time to time. Sprinkle lightly with pepper immediately before serving.

LEBERKNÖDEL

If you have been to Germany you know what a Leberknödel is. If you haven't it is about as easy to describe as a banana. You can tell somebody what it looks like, but just try and tell them how it tastes. They are about the size of a tennisball and are served as a main dish, in beef bouillon as a main dish, or in soup before a meal.

1/2 lb. calf's liver
1 egg
3/4 lb. stale white bread
1 medium onion
1 pint milk
1/2 level teaspoon baking powder
lard or shortening (to fry onions)
1-1/2 rounded tablespoons flour
2 rounded tablespoons chopped parsley

1 level teaspoon marjoram
1 level teaspoon salt

Cut stale bread including crusts in very thin slices, about 1/16 inch thick. Pour heated, but not boiled, milk over stale bread and let sit for 1 hour. Chop onion. Fry onion and parsley until onion is glassy. Set aside.

Cut liver in strips and grind twice. After the bread has soaked for 1 hour fill a large soup pot one-half full of salted water and bring to a rolling boil. Add all the ingredients to the soaked bread and knead to a uniform consistency. The dough must be well mixed so that no chunks or pieces of bread remain.

With wet hands form a Knödel (ball), about the size of a tennisball and drop into the boiling water. Dip hands in cold water after making each Knödel and repeat to make a total of six Knödels and medium boil, covered, for 20 minutes. Remove and serve hot.

BAUERNSCHMAUS

Translated, Bauernschmaus is a "Farmers' Feast" and I always think of it in an enormous farm kitchen with a steaming wood stove, a scrubbed white pine table two inches thick and the head of the household saying "Mahlzeit" (an expression which cannot be translated in English but roughly means in this case "enjoy your meal") as the wooden plates are served.

Typical Menu: Bauernschmaus — I won't even try to describe this
Schwarzbrot — Black bread
Bier — Beer

1-3/4 lbs. cooked pork, rather fat
6 Leberknödel, see pg. 74
6 pork sausages
6 slices smoked bacon about 1/8 inch thick
Sauerkraut, see pg. 122

mashed potatoes
hot German mustard

Heat Knōdels in boiling water. Cut pork in six slices. Heat kraut and pork together. Heat mashed potatoes. Fry sausage and bacon. On each wooden plate place a generous helping of mashed potatoes, sauerkraut, a Leberknōdel, a slice of pork, one sausage and a slice of bacon. Serve with hot mustard.

SAURE LEBER

Saure Leber is a favorite in all of Germany and is found on practically all the menus of all the Gasthauses. If your husband doesn't like it, tell him it is an old German favorite, which will guarantee keeping him from running off with the cute German cook who works in the restaurant down on the corner. If he does like it, it's the best way to guarantee keeping him from running off with the cute German cook who works in the restaurant down on the corner. You haven't got a thing to lose.

Typical Menu: Suppe -- Soup
                     Saure Leber -- Liver in brown gravy
                     Kartoffelpuree -- Mashed potatoes
                     Gruner Salat -- Green salad

1 3/4 lbs. pork or calf's liver
3 rounded tablespoons butter or lard
I medium onion

3 cups boiling water
1 1/2 tablespoons vinegar
1 1/2 rounded teaspoon flour
1 1/2 level teaspoons salt
1/8 teaspoon pepper

Cut liver in slices about 3/16 inch thick. Then cut in cubes about 1 inch square. (I usually let the butcher do this as I just can't stand to touch the crawly stuff.) Cut onions in thin rings, then cut rings in halves and quarters. Melt fat in a pan, add liver cubes and brown both sides very lightly. Add onion rings and flour. Stir well with a fork to blend flour with hot fat. Brown liver to a light brown. Add boiling (important -- cold water will make the liver tough) water and vinegar. Stir well with a fork or egg whisk to prevent lumps. Do not salt. Cover pan and simmer on low heat for 30 minutes. Add salt and pepper after removing from stove immediately before serving.

PFALZ FORTRESS
ON A RHINE ISLAND

Fisch und Geflügel

Fish and Fowl

Recipes to serve six

FORELLE NACH MÜLLERIN ART

A MÜLLER ist a miller, a MÜLLERIN is the miller's wife. So it doesn't take too much imagination to see why trout turned in flour then fried is called "Trout in the style of the miller's wife".

Typical Menu: Suppe — Soup, optional
                      Forelle nach Müllerin Art — Fried trout
                      Petersilbutter — Parsley butter, see pg. 153
                      Petersilkartoffeln — Parsley potatoes

6 fresh trout, each between 3/4 and 1 lb.   flour
butter   3 lemons

Clean and rinse the trout in cold running water. Dry with a towel. Sprinkle with lemon juice and turn in flour until well coated. Fry in hot butter until done. Serve on prewarmed plates with lemon slices and parsley butter.

FORELLEN IN WEISSWEIN

Typical Menu: Suppe — Soup, asparagus or cauliflower go well
                         Forellen in Weisswein — Trout in white wine sauce
                         Pellkartoffeln — Boiled new potatoes

6 fresh trout, each about 3/4 to 1 lb.
  or 6 frozen trout
6 small tomatoes
4 scallions

2 cups white wine, preferably dry
1-1/2 cups Hollandaise sauce, see pg. 148
4-5 sprigs of tarragon
salt

Cut tomatoes in quarters and cut scallions crosswise in rings. Place cleaned trout, tomatoes, scallions and tarragon leaves in a casserole. Add wine and simmer until half done, covered, about 7 minutes, longer for frozen trout. Very carefully turn the trout and cook until done, then carefully lift trout from the casserole, remove heads, tails and skin. Place on prewarmed plates in a warm oven. Bring the sauce remaining in the casserole to a rapid boil and mash in the tomatoes. Strain through a fine sieve. Add the Hollandaise, salt to taste, pour over the fish, serve.

FISCH-FRIKADELLEN

Fisch-Frikadellen are the hamburgers of the North Sea coast.

Typical Menu: Fisch-Frikadellen — Fish cakes
                  Kartoffelsalat — Potato salad, cold
                  Katsup — Catsup

2-1/2 lbs. cooked fish, any kind
5 slices of stale white bread
5 eggs
1-1/2 rounded tablespoons flour

1-1/2 cups bread crumbs
1-1/2 level teaspoons salt
shortening or fat, any kind

Pluck the fish into very small pieces. Dip the bread in water and squeeze out. Knead fish, bread, 3 eggs, flour and salt together to a uniform dough. Beat the remaining 2 eggs. Form twelve cakes from the fish, dip in beaten egg, then in bread crumbs and fry in hot fat to a golden brown.

RETURNING WITH
THE DAYS CATCH FROM
THE NORTH SEA

AAL IN ASPIK

This recipe is for eel, but can be used with any other fish. Good for a cold dinner or for a buffet.

Typical Menu: Aal in Aspik — Eel in aspic
Tomatenscheiben — Tomato wedges
Mayonnaise — Mayonnaise

3 to 4 lbs. eel
2-1/2 quarts water
1 cup vinegar
1 onion
3 bay leaves
clear gelatin, enough for 1 quart liquid
2 egg whites

2 egg shells
2 lemons
6 hard-boiled eggs
2 large pickles
2 carrots
salt
pepper

Wash and clean eel. Cut in slices about 1/2 inch thick. Peel and slice onion.

Bring water to a boil, add bay leaves, carrots, onion slices, and vinegar. Salt to taste, add eel and simmer until done. Remove from water, drain. Remove carrots from water, drain. Retain 1 quart of the water.

Remove bones and skin from the eel slices, sprinkle with salt, pepper and lemon juice and let marinate for 1/2 hour. Crush the egg shells. Beat the egg whites to soft peaks together with the egg shells. Bring the retained fish water almost to a boil and add the egg whites and shells, stirring constantly with an egg whisk. Remove from stove, cover and let stand until the egg white has cooked and the water is clear. Skim off the scum and filter through a clean cloth. Dissolve gelatin according to instructions on the package and add to hot fish water.

Rub a casserole lightly with butter and pour in about 1/4 inch liquid, but not hot, aspic. Place in refrigerator and let set. Do not freeze.

Slice the hard-boiled eggs, the carrots and the pickles. Arrange the pieces of eel, egg slices, carrot slices and pickle slices on the set aspic. Pour remaining aspic, liquid but not warm, over the contents. Chill in refrigerator until set. Dip casserole in hot water and invert. Garnish with mayonnaise and tomato slices.

ENTE MIT KASTANIENFÜLLUNG

Roast duck, either wild or domestic, stuffed with roasted chestnuts will establish your reputation as a cook in any circle.

Typical Menu: Suppe — Soup
Ente mit Kastanienfüllung — Roast duck with chestnut filling
Kartoffelpüree — Mashed potatoes
Blaukraut — Red cabbage, see pg. 125

| 2 ducks | salt |
| 2 lbs. chestnuts | pepper |

Pluck, clean and singe ducks. Boil chestnuts until the shells and skins can be removed. Rub duck inside and out with salt and pepper, stuff with chestnuts and sew shut. Roast in 350° oven, basting frequently until done, about 2 hours. If gravy is desired, prepare as for Ente nach Bayerischer Art on pg. 90.

ELTZ CASTLE

GEBRATENE ENTE NACH BAYERISCHER ART

As you have gathered from my comments, the Bavarians are the best cooks in Germany. This recipe just goes to prove it.

Typical Menu: Leberknödelsuppe — See pg. 102
Gebratene Ente — Roast duck
Kartoffelknödel — Potato dumplings, see pg. 118
Blaukraut — Red cabbage, see pg. 125
Bier — Beer or Weisswein — White wine

1 large duck	2 medium onions
2 lbs. fairly lean pork	2 or 3 bunches of parsley
2 pints soup stock	salt
1 rounded tablespoon lard	pepper
2 rounded tablespoons flour	

Pluck, clean and singe duck. Cut pork in six slices or pieces. Peel onion and cut in wedges about 1/4 inch thick lengthwise. Rub duck inside and out with salt and pepper. Place duck, pork, onion wedges and lard in roasting pan. Put pan in hot, 350° oven. As soon as duck begins to brown, pour 1/2 cup boiling water over it. Repeat this frequently, but not so often that the water is over 1/4 inch deep in the bottom of the pan. When duck is a golden brown, cover pan, continue basting with boiling water and cook until done. Remove the duck from pan and with the pastry brush paint the skin lightly with ice water. This makes the skin crisp. Remove pan from oven, place duck on rack and return to oven for 5 to 10 minutes until skin is crisp.

Place pan on stove, remove pork, pour off grease and keep liquid boiling. Add flour to pan, stirring well to prevent lumps. Add boiling soup stock, salt and pepper to taste. Simmer 5 minutes, stirring well to dissolve brown from bottom of pan. Cut duck into serving size-pieces with poultry shears. Serve duck and pork on a large prewarmed platter garnished with parsley. Strain gravy and serve separately in a gravy boat.

WACHTELN

The air was crisp and cool and the first of the falling leaves crunched under my feet as I walked the last thirty meters out of the forest into the clearing. Suddenly a brace of quail flushed from almost under my feet. I raised my double barrel and fired twice in rapid sequence. I got both. Three tail feathers from one and two tail feathers from the other. Picking up six quail at the Zerwirkgewölbe, the oldest game market in Munich, and removing the price tags I returned home after a hard day's gunning.

Typical Menu: Flädlesuppe — Pancake soup, see pg. 103
Wachteln — Quail
Kartoffelpüree — Mashed potatoes
Spargel — Asparagus

6 quail
6 thin, as thin as you can slice it, slices of pork fat or unsalted sowbelly as big as
    your hand

1/4 lb. butter, no substitute
6 large grape leaves
1 cup fresh juniper berries
2 cups white wine
1 rounded tablespoon flour
salt
pepper
thread

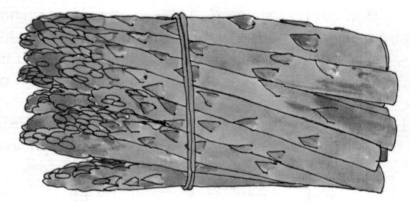

Pluck, clean and singe quail. Rub inside and out with salt, pepper and juniper berries, crushing the berries as you rub, so the juice penetrates the skin.

Wrap each quail with a grape leaf, then with the pork fat. Bind with thread. Fry in hot butter until done. Remove quail from pan. Stir in flour and let brown slightly. Stir in wine. Salt and pepper to taste. This will give a small amount of very rich gravy. Serve hot.

GEBRATENER FASAN

Don't forget to remove the price tags after shooting pheasant, (like I do) and, oh yes, possibly insert a bird shot or two in the skin with a sharply pointed knife. A guest might loose a tooth, but that's why you have insurance, and it makes the story of the hunt so much more poignant . . . and believeable.

Typical Menu: Champignoncreme-Suppe — Cream of mushroom soup
                        Gebratener Fasan — Roast pheasant
                        Pellkartoffeln — New potatoes
                        Sauerkraut — Sauerkraut

2 pheasants
2 large, very thin, as thin as possible, slices of pork fat or unsalted sow belly. They should be as large as a sheet of paper. If you can't get them this large get smaller slices to cover the same area.

4 bunches of parsley
butter
salt
pepper

Cut wings from pheasants, spread and straighten the feathers. Retain for future use. Pluck, clean and singe pheasants. Rub inside and out with salt and pepper. Wrap pheasants with pork fat slices and bind in place with thread. Roast pheasants on rotisserie with medium high heat, basting frequently with hot (important—hot) butter until done, about 45 to 50 minutes.

Remove thread and place the pheasants breast up on a large prewarmed serving tray. Ring tray with new potatoes sprinkled with melted butter and finely chopped parsley. Garnish with bunches of parsley. Place the wings, spread, on each side of the pheasants.

Suppen

Soups

Recipes to serve six

FLEISCHBRÜHE (Soup Stock)

Fleischbrühe is the basic soup stock for the recipes found herein. Served alone it is an excellent beef bouillon. Used as the basis for soups and sauces it adds that flavor you just can't get from a bouillon cube.

a handful of soup bones, (beef) and a marrow bone
1-1/2 lbs. soup meat
4 quarts water
1 rounded tablespoon salt
1 medium onion

2 carrots
1 bunch parsley
3 or 4 strips leek
1 piece celery

Wash bones and meat. Remove only the brown outer skin from onion. Wash vegetables. Add all the ingredients to the pot and cold water. Bring to a slow boil. Skim off the brown scum that forms. Simmer slowly for 2 hours, skimming off scum from time to time. Remove from stove and strain through a dish towel or white cloth. Salt and pepper to taste.

NUDELSUPPE MIT RINDFLEISCH NACH BAUERNART

This is not the beef noodle soup that you would be served in Munich or on the Kurfürstendamm in Berlin on a starched white cloth set with china and crystal. This is the beef noodle soup you will find in a Gasthaus, in an Alpen pass, with scrubbed white pine tables, earthenware, a pot-bellied stove glowing in the corner as the blizzard howls outside. The quantities given here are for a main dish.

3-1/2 qts. Fleischbrühe and beef and vegetables cooked with it.
1 lb. wide egg noodles
2 teaspoons oil
1-1/2 level tablespoons lard, fat or shortening
2 level tablespoons flour
1/2 level tablespoon ground, not powdered, marjoram
salt
pepper

noodles in boiling salted water, to which 2 teaspoons of oil have been added before boiling over, for 10 minutes. Drain.

Cut meat in small chunks about 1/4 inch square. Remove and discard all fat and sinews. Finely chop carrot, onion, parsley, leek, and celery. Melt fat in soup pot and stir in flour. Simmer slowly about 5 minutes until it begins to brown. Add boiling soup stock slowly, stirring constantly to prevent lumps. Add all remaining ingredients and simmer slowly about 45 minutes. Serve almost boiling in big, deep soup bowls with black bread and butter.

KARTOFFELSUPPE (German Potato Soup)

This can be served as a soup before the meal or as a one dish dinner. As a one dish dinner, double the quantities and serve in deep soup bowls with black bread, butter and a salad.

2 strips lean bacon

3—3-1/4 lbs. potatoes

1/2 small onion
2 slightly rounded tablespoons lard,
   no substitute
2 level tablespoons flour
2-3/4 pints soup stock

3/4 level teaspoon ground,
   not powdered, marjoram
2-3 sprigs parsley
1 sprig celery leaves
salt and pepper

Cook whole peeled potatoes in salted water about 30 minutes until done, but still firm, not mushy. Remove from pot. Pour out water. Finely chop bacon, onion, parsley, and celery. Melt lard in pot. Fry bacon and onions until they begin to brown. Stir in flour with a fork. Simmer for another minute or two. Add parsley and celery. Add marjoram, powdering it between your fingers as you add it to the pot. Add soup stock slowly, stirring constantly, with a fork to prevent lumps. Simmer 15 minutes covered.

Mash 2/3 of the potatoes and dice the remaining 1/3. Stir mashed potatoes into simmering soup and add diced potatoes. Salt and pepper to taste. Let simmer an additional 10 minutes and serve.

LEBERKNÖDELSUPPE

This is the favorite soup in Bavaria. For an explanation of Leberknödel see pg. 74.

3-1/2 pints soup stock, (If Knodel are to be cooked in soup, 2 quarts)
6 Leberknödel, 12 if the soup is the main dish
2 rounded tablespoons finely chopped chives

If Leberknödel are already prepared, place them in soup, bring to simmer. Remove from stove, let sit for 5 minutes. Serve in deep soup bowls garnished with chives.

If Leberknödel must be prepared, prepare them according to the recipe on page 74 and cook Leberknödel in soup stock 20 to 30 minutes. Serve in deep soup bowls garnished with chives.

PFANNKUCHENSUPPE or FLÄDELSUPPE or FRIDATTENSUPPE
(Pancake Soup)

3-1/2 pints soup stock
1-1/2 level cups flour
2 cups milk
2 eggs
1 teaspoon salt
lard
1/3 cup finely chopped chives

Beat flour, milk, eggs and salt together well to make a thin batter.

Warm frying pan and rub with lard, then wipe out with a paper towel. Dip batter into hot frying pan or griddle to make pancakes about 8 inches in diameter. Cook to a golden brown on both sides. Put pancakes in freezer or refrigerator to cool for 1/2 hour. Cut pancakes in thin strips not quite as wide as a pencil and divide equally in soup bowls. Pour in boiling hot soup stock and garnish with chopped chives.

BACKERBSENSUPPE

"Pea" soup, with peas that come from the baker — not from the farmer. If you were in Germany you could buy Backerbsen at any market. But since you are not, you will have to make them like Grandma did.

3-1/2 pints soup stock
1/3 cup finely chopped chives

For the Backerbsen:
1/2 pint milk
1-3/4 cup flour
2 tablespoons lard or shortening
1 egg
3/4 teaspoon salt
lard, shortening, or vegetable oil to deep fat fry

The Backerbsen: Make a batter of the ingredients for the Backerbsen and put into a pastry tube. Squeeze out small drops about the size of a pea into the cooking deep fat. Fry to a golden brown. They will expand to the size of a marble. Dip out with a sieve, drain, set aside to cool. Continue until all the batter is used.

The soup: Bring soup to a boil, remove from heat, add Backerbsen, cover and let sit 3 to 5 minutes. Garnish with chives and serve.

BROTSUPPE

This recipe for bread soup comes from the Allgäu close to the Austrian border. I wish that you could see the Tyrolean Alps out of your kitchen window as you are cooking it.

3/4 lb. unsliced rye bread
3-1/2 pints soup stock
1 medium onion
1/4 lb. liverwurst
2 medium potatoes

1/2 level teaspoon ground,
      not powdered, marjoram, optional
salt
pepper

Slice the bread very thin and save three or four days until stale. Peel potatoes and slice in thin slices. Peel onion, leave whole. Put the stale bread, potato slices, whole onion and liverwurst in the soup pot. Add marjoram, if desired, powdering it between your fingers. Pour in boiling soup stock. Simmer slowly 1/2 to 3/4 hour, stirring occasionally to break up bread and mix in liverwurst. Salt and pepper to taste. Serve HOT.

EINLAUFSUPPE

Einlaufsuppe is similar to Chinese egg drop soup. One of the light soups, it is ideal before a heavy meal.

3-1/2 pints soup stock
2 eggs
2 level tablespoons flour
1/8 teaspoon salt
2 tablespoons finely chopped parsley
    or
2 tablespoons finely chopped chives

Beat eggs, flour and salt together well. Bring soup to a slow boil. Add egg mixture to soup, stirring constantly with the egg whisk so that long threads of egg are formed. After all of egg mixture is added simmer slowly 2 to 3 minutes. Garnish with chopped parsley or chives.

BLUMENKOHLSUPPE (Cream of Cauliflower Soup)

1 medium head cauliflower
2 level tablespoons shortening or butter
6 level tablespoons flour
1 egg yolk

1 cup heavy cream
salt
1/3 cup finely chopped chives
3-1/2 pints water

Wash and clean cauliflower. Cut flowers from cauliflower head and soak in cold salted water 15 minutes. Drain. In a large soup pot bring the water to a boil. Put cauliflower in water. Cover, cook for 5 minutes. Do not overcook. Remove cauliflower from water. Pour water in an alternate pot and retain for later use.

Melt shortening in soup pot and stir in flour. Simmer slowly, stirring often, 3 to 5 minutes. Do not brown. Add retained water, stirring with a fork or egg whisk to prevent lumps. Salt to taste. Simmer slowly, covered, 20 minutes. Beat egg yolk with cream and place in soup tureen. Add soup to the tureen, stirring into egg and cream with egg whisk. Add cauliflower to soup. Garnish with chopped chives.

HALLSTATT

SQUEEZED BETWEEN
MOUNTAIN AND LAKE

TOMATENSUPPE (Cream of Tomato Soup)

This tastes just a little bit different from any tomato soup you have ever eaten.

2 quarts soup stock
1/2 medium onion
2 level tablespoons lard or shortening
6 level tablespoons flour
1 rounded teaspoon finely chopped parsley
3 rounded tablespoons triple concentrated tomato paste
1/4 level teaspoon sugar
1/2 teaspoon vinegar
1 lemon
salt
pepper

Cook finely chopped onion in melted lard until it is glassy. Do not brown. Add flour and stir in with a fork. Simmer slowly until onions are brown. Add boiling soup stock slowly, stirring constantly with a fork or an egg whisk to prevent lumps. Stir in parsley, tomato paste, sugar, and vinegar. Salt to taste. Simmer slowly, covered, for 20 minutes. Slice six paper thin slices from the lemon. Strain soup through sieve. Sprinkle soup with pepper and float a lemon slice in each bowl just before serving.

GRIESS-SUPPE

In Germany you would use griess, which is wheat, but in America you can use hominy grits.

2 quarts soup stock
9 tablespoons uncooked hominy grits
1/4 teaspoon marjoram
1 egg, optional
2 tablespoons finely chopped parsley

Bring soup to a boil. Add marjoram. Stir in grits and cover. Cook slowly for 20 minutes. If egg is used, beat well and stir into soup with an egg whisk immediately before serving. Garnish with parsley.

GRIESSNOCKERLSUPPE ("Grits Dumpling" Soup)

See description of Griess on preceding page.

2 quarts soup stock
3/4 cups of uncooked hominy grits
1 tablespoon butter or margarine
1 egg
1/8 level teaspoon salt

1 teaspoon finely chopped parsley, optional
2 tablespoons chopped parsley
  or
2 tablespoons finely chopped chives

Bring the soup to a boil. Mix the grits, butter, egg, salt and parsley, if desired, together in a mixing bowl. Immediately after mixing, cut Nockerls, small dumplings, from the mixture with a teaspoon. Now this will be a little difficult to describe. They are the right size and shape if they fit between two teaspoons placed bowl to bowl together. Or in other words the size of a flat pigeon's egg.

Drop these into the cooking soup. (They will expand while cooking to the size of a small egg.) Cover. Simmer for 20 minutes, remove from stove and let sit for another 10 minutes before serving. Garnish with parsley or chives.

SCHOKOLADENSUPPE (Chocolate Soup)

In Northern Germany, particularly Bremen, Hamburg and Oldenburg, "sweet" soups are frequently served before a meal, which is a little unusual to Americans, to say the least.

3-1/2 pints milk
3 rounded tablespoons cocoa
1-1/2 rounded tablespoons cornstarch

1-1/2 cup sugar
2 egg whites

Add 1 to 2 tablespoons of sugar to the egg whites and beat until they form stiff peaks. Blend cocoa and cornstarch with 1/2 pint cold milk. Bring the remaining 3 pints of milk to a boil. Stir in the cocoa, cornstarch, milk mixture, and remaining sugar. Cook slowly 3 to 5 minutes. Float spoonfuls of the egg whites on the soup. Remove from heat, cover and let sit for 5 minutes. The spoonfuls of egg white can also be added to the soup in a soup tureen. If so, cover and let sit 5 minutes.

RIVER TRAFFIC GOING
PAST CAT CASTLE

Gemüse und Knödel

Vegetables and Knödel

Recipes to serve six

KARTOFFELKNÖDEL (Untranslatable)

Kartoffelknödel are "potato dumplings" about the size of a tennis ball. It would be a black Sunday in a real Bavarian household if there weren't Kartoffelknödel on the table to go with the Schweinebraten. They are wonderful.

6 lbs. large (they're easier to grate) potatoes
2 eggs
1 rounded tablespoon flour
1 level teaspoon salt
2 slices white bread
butter
1 tablespoon vinegar
1/4 to 1/2 teaspoons sulfur

Cook 2 lbs. of the potatoes. Drain and let cool. Peel remaining potatoes and place in a large pot. Put the sulfur in an old saucer, set the saucer on the raw potatoes and light. Cover the pot tightly and let sit 15 minutes; (this bleaches the potatoes, otherwise the Knodel won't be snow white).

Remove potatoes and finely grate into a bowl with water and vinegar. Squeeze out grated potatoes as much as possible in a dish towel. Peel cooked potatoes and grate. Cut bread into 1/4 inch squares and fry in butter.

Mix raw and cooked potatoes and other ingredients well. Form six balls as big as baseballs with 5 or 6 bread squares in the middle of each. Cook in boiling water 15 to 20 minutes. Do not overcook as they will fall apart. Drain and serve hot. They're work, but boy they're good. Mmmmmm!

KARTOFFELKÜCHLEIN

These are sometimes called potato pancakes by Americans.

2 lbs. potatoes	1/3 cup flour	lard, shortening,
2 eggs	1 level teaspoon salt	butter or margarine to fry

Cook and peel potatoes 1 to 2 days ahead or use leftover potatoes. Mash potatoes until smooth. Mix with other ingredients. With damp hands form small balls and pat into thin pancakes. Fry in hot fat until brown.

KARTOFFELPUFFER or REIBEDATSCHI – These are the real potato pancakes.

2 lbs. large potatoes	2 eggs	lard, or shortening to fry
1 onion	1 level teaspoon salt	

Peel potatoes. Finely grate onions and potatoes and mix with other ingredients. Drop by spoonfuls into hot fat. Form thin cakes and fry until crisp.

SALZKARTOFFELN NACH BAYERISCHER ART
(Bavarian Style Boiled Potatoes)

12 medium potatoes, enough for six persons
salt
1 level tablespoon lard or fat
1 medium onion

Wash and peel potatoes. Place in cold water as soon as peeled to prevent their turning brown. Cut potatoes in chunks about the size of a walnut. Cook potatoes in salted water until tender, about 20 minutes. Cut onion in half, then into very thin rings. Fry onion until dark brown. Remove potatoes from pot, place in serving dish, and pour fried onions and grease over potatoes. Serve.

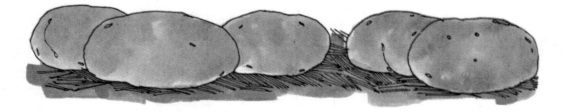

MILLER'S SAUERKRAUT

As the Italians are called "Spaghetti benders" and the French "frogs" (frog eaters), Germans didn't come by the name "Krauts" accidentally. Germans consume it by the thousands of tons in every way, shape and form. The most favorite of which is sauerkraut.

2 lbs. fresh sauerkraut from the barrel, or
2 one pound cans sauerkraut, three if not tightly packed
1/4 lb. fairly fat pork or sow belly, optional
1-1/2 tablespoons lard, no substitutes
1 medium onion
18 dried juniper berries
2 level teaspoons salt
1 rounded tablespoon flour
1 apple
1 medium potato
1/4 cup cold water

Wash and drain the sauerkraut. Simmer the kraut slowly in hot lard for about 5 minutes, turning often with a fork until it has absorbed the melted lard.

When using fresh sauerkraut, add boiling water and salt. Cover. Simmer slowly two hours, proceed as below.

When using canned sauerkraut, add boiling water and salt. Proceed Immediately as below.

Peel onion, leave whole. Peel and slice apple. Salt pork. Add pork, onion, apple and juniper berries to Kraut. Simmer slowly, covered, 1 hour or until pork is done.

Mix flour with 1/4 cup cold water. Peel and finely grate potato. Add flour/water mixture and potato. Mix well. Simmer for an additional 10 to 15 minutes. Salt to taste.

BAYERISCHES KRAUT (Bavarian Style Cabbage)

1 large head white cabbage
1-1/2 tablespoons lard, no substitute
1 small onion
2 level teaspoons caraway seeds
salt

Cut cabbage in half and grate exactly as if you were going to make cole slaw. Peel and finely chop onion. Melt lard in pot. Add onions and simmer until glassy. Add grated cabbage. Simmer slowly, turning frequently with a fork until fat is absorbed, about 5 minutes. Do not brown. Add caraway seeds, salt lightly and add a very little water to make steam. Cover. Cook slowly until tender, about 1/2 hour.

BLAUKRAUT or ROTKOHL (Red Cabbage)

1 large head of red cabbage
1-1/2 tablespoons lard or shortening
1 medium onion
2 bay leaves, whole
10 cloves

2 tablespoons vinegar
1-2 large apples
1/2 teaspoons sugar
1 teaspoon cornstarch
salt

Cut cabbage in quarters and cut out stem. Grate cabbage fairly fine. Finely dice the onion. Melt lard in a large pot and lightly brown onions. Add grated cabbage and stir until fat is absorbed. Add bay leaves, cloves, vinegar, sugar, and a little water to steam. Steam, covered, for 1/2 hour. Peel and core apples. Slice in slices about 1/4 thick. Add apples, salt to taste and steam an additional 1/2 hour. Mix cornstarch with a little cold water. If there is about a cup of water remaining in the pot add cornstarch-water mixture and stir in. If not, add water. Remove bay leaves and serve.

ROSENKOHL (Brussels Sprouts)

The word for word translation of Rosenkohl would be rose cabbage which is really much more poetic than Brussels sprouts. (My apologies to any Belgians I have just offended.)

2-3 lbs. Brussels sprouts or enough for six servings
2 level tablespoons butter
3 level tablespoons flour
1/8 tablespoon freshly grated nutmeg
2 tablespoons heavy cream
salt
4 cups water

Clean Brussels sprouts, removing withered outer leaves and cutting off stems. Soak in salted water 15 minutes. Drain. In a large pot bring 4 cups of salted water to a boil. Add Brussels sprouts, cover, steam for 5 minutes. Drain Brussels sprouts in colander, retaining water in a smaller pot for later use.

Melt butter in large pot. Stir in flour with a fork. Simmer slowly 5 minutes. Do not allow to brown. Add retained water slowly, stirring with a fork to prevent lumps. Salt to taste. Add nutmeg, heavy cream and stir. Cover and simmer slowly 15 minutes. Add Brussels sprouts. Simmer for an additional 2 to 3 minutes.

ÜBERBACKENER BLUMENKOHL (Baked Cauliflower)

1 large head of cauliflower or two smaller heads
2 tablespoons butter, no substitute
2 tablespoons flour
1/4 level teaspoon salt
pepper
1/2 cup grated cheese, Emmentaler, Cheddar, or Parmesan
3 strips bacon
1/2 cup bread crumbs fried in butter

Cut green leaves from the base of the cauliflower being careful to leave the full head intact. Wash and soak in salt water 15 minutes.

Pour about 2 inches of water in a large pot and bring to a boil. Place the cauliflower head upright in the boiling water, cover, and cook for 5 to 7 minutes, until you can insert a fork, but not tender. Remove cauliflower carefully from water and set aside to drain. Retain water.

Preheat oven to 400°. Rub a casserole with grease and set aside.

Melt butter in a small frying pan, add flour and stir in. Cook until it begins to brown, stirring constantly. Add 2 cups of the water retained from cooking the cauliflower and stir in well with a fork or egg whisk. Cook until the mixture thickens. Add salt and pepper.

Place cauliflower head upright in casserole and pour sauce over cauliflower. Sprinkle with grated cheese and pepper. Add bacon strips. Bake in 400° oven 20 to 30 minutes until browned over, or bake 20 minutes and brown under broiler. Sprinkle fried bread crumbs over cauliflower immediately before serving.

GEBACKENER BLUMENKOHL (Fried Cauliflower)

This recipe can also be used with carrots, small firm tomatoes, Brussels sprouts, artichoke hearts, celery or Schwarzwurzeln. Deeeelicious!

1 large head of cauliflower
1 level cup flour
2 eggs
1/2 cup milk

1-1/2 teaspoons melted butter
salt
shortening to fry

Wash cauliflower and cut individual flowers from stalk. Soak in salt water 15 minutes. Drain. Put 2 inches of water in pot, add 2 teaspoons salt and bring to boil. Cook cauliflower not over 5 minutes, until you can insert a fork, but not until tender and remove from water and drain.

Prepare a batter as follows: Sieve the flour, stir in milk, melted butter, egg, and 3/4 teaspoon salt. Mix well so that no lumps remain. Spear cauliflower with a fork, dip into batter, coat well, and drop in hot deep fat. Fry to a golden brown. As they are done remove from fat and drain.

LEIPZIGER ALLERLEI (Mixed Vegetables)

The secret of this recipe is not to overcook . . . tender, just barely tender.

1/2 lb. fresh green peas
1/2 lb. fresh garden carrots
1/2 lb. fresh asparagus
2 kohlrabi
1 medium head cauliflower
1 rounded tablespoon finely chopped parsley

1/8 lb. butter or margarine
3 tablespoons sifted flour
1/2 teaspoon sugar
salt
pepper

Clean carrots. Peel asparagus and cut in 2-inch long pieces. Peel and slice kohlrabi. Cut flowers from cauliflower and soak in salt water 15 minutes.

Melt butter in a pot. Add peas, carrots, asparagus, kohlrabi, and parsley. Simmer very slowly, covered, 5 minutes. Sift flour over simmering vegetables. Stir in. Add 1 cup water and sugar. Salt and pepper to taste. Simmer until done, about 30 minutes. In another pot cook cauliflower in salted water until tender, about 7 minutes. Add cauliflower to the other vegetables just before serving.

CULTIVATING
THE
VINEYARDS

M.NELSON

$\mathfrak{Salate}$

Salads

This section is extremely difficult to write. It is a beautiful spring morning. Outside my window the sky is blue through the cherry blossoms, the grass is green, the lawn is a marshalling ground for tiny spring flowers, the sender from Vienna is playing Viennese waltzes . . . the world is a wonderful place to live, especially in the spring, expecially in Bavaria, especially in Munich. It's too beautiful a day, I'll write this later.

Later. Of course we get lettuce and salads during winter, but there is nothing like the taste of fresh salad, fresh from the gardener, in the spring. These are the salads we find in Germany.

133

KARTOFFELSALAT

I. Hot potato salad:
   3 lbs. potatoes
   1-1/4 cups soup stock
   1 large onion
   4-6 strips bacon
   1/3 cup salad oil, not olive oil
   2 tablespoons vinegar
   salt and pepper

Wash and cook potatoes, not too done as they should still be firm. Peel and mince onion. Cut bacon crosswise in 1/4 inch lengths. Fry until crisp. Drain. Peel potatoes while still warm and slice 1/8 inch thick. Add bacon, minced onion, oil, vinegar and hot soup stock. Salt and pepper to taste. Let marinate 1 hour. Serve hot.

II. Potato salad:
   3 lbs. potatoes
   1-1/4 cups soup stock
   1 large onion
   1/3 cup salad oil, not olive oil
   2-1/2 tablespoons vinegar
   1 bunch parsley, chopped fine
   salt and pepper

Wash and cook potatoes, not too done as they should still be firm. Peel and mince onion. Peel potatoes while still warm and cut in slices about 1/8 inch thick. Pour hot soup stock over potatoes. Let cool. Whip vinegar and oil together and add to salad. Add other ingredients. Mix well. Let stand at least 2 hours. Salt and pepper to taste. Serve cool. Add mayonnaise if desired.

CHICOREESALAT (Chicory Salad)

Clean chicory and remove stem. Let sit ten minutes in lightly salted hot water. Drain, cool, cut crosswise strips as for cole slaw. Oil, lemon juice, salt, pepper, a pinch of sugar and a little minced onion.

KRESSESALAT (Cress Salad)

Wash and drain. Oil, vinegar or lemon juice, salt and pepper.

ENDIVIENSALAT (Endive Salad)

Wash endive. Cut in strips as for cole slaw. Let sit in hot water 10 minutes to remove bitterness. Drain. Oil, lemon juice or vinegar, salt and pepper. Minced onion, optional. Often mixed with chicory.

GRUNER BOHNENSALAT (Green Bean Salad)

Wash string or snap beans and remove strings. Cut in pieces about 1 inch long. Cook in salt water with a piece of pork or a strip of bacon and some savory, optional. Drain. Mix with minced onion, oil, lemon juice or vinegar, salt, pepper and a pinch of sugar while still hot. Let marinate 1/2 hour. Cool and serve.

GURKENSALAT (Cucumber Salad)

Peel cucumber and cut in slices about 1/8 inch thick. Oil, lemon juice or vinegar, salt and rather heavy pepper. Also served with cream salad dressings. Dill and minced onion or onion rings optional. Frequently used in mixed salads or with potato salad.

KRAUTSALAT (Kraut Salad)

Wash Kraut and grate as for cole slaw. Put in large pot. Cover with boiling water. Cover, let sit for five minutes. Drain. Fry bacon chips with diced onions. Let cool. Mix bacon, onions, oil, vinegar, caraway seeds and salt and pepper with Kraut. Let marinate 1 hour. Serve cold.

PAPRIKASALAT (Bell Pepper Salad)

I. Pickled paprika — use as is.

II. Fresh Paprika — Wash, remove stem and seeds. Cut in strips. Marinate in oil, vinegar, salt and pepper 1/2 hour.

III. Cooked paprika — Wash, remove stem and seeds. Cut in strips. Cook in salt water until not quite tender. Drain. Marinate in oil, vinegar, salt and pepper. Serve cold.

ROTER RÜBENSALAT (Red Beet Salad)

I. Pickled beets — Use as is with a few onion rings.

II. Pickled beets, do it yourself — Cut tops from beets and brush clean in running water. Cook until tender, about 1-1/2 hours, in salt water. Quench with cold water to make peeling easier. Peel. Marinate in: vinegar and water 1:1, with salt, a little sugar, onion rings and a little horseradish. Marinate 3 days. Serve with a few onion rings.

SAUERKRAUTSALAT (Sauerkraut Salad)

Mix onion rings or finely minced onion with cooked sauerkraut. See page 122. Add salt, oil and vinegar. Marinate 1 day. Caraway seeds, or fried bacon, optional. Serve hot or cold.

HALLSTATT

KRABBENSALAT (Shrimp Salad)

Cook and clean shrimp or wash and drain canned shrimp. Mix with mayonnaise. Spice with celery salt, dill. Optional: Chopped boiled eggs, chopped celery, chopped pickles, or minced onion. Let marinate 1 hour. Serve cold.

FISCHSALAT (Fish Salad)

Cooked fish, any kind. Remove skin and bones. Pluck into small pieces. Mix with mayonnaise, minced onion, minced pickles, a little lemon juice and a little hot mustard. Optional: Chopped boiled eggs, chopped celery. Decorate with parsley, chives, dill or paprika. Let marinate 1 hour. Serve cold.

FLEISCHSALAT ("Meat" Salad)

I. Cooked meat. Cut in small strips about 1 inch long. Mix with chopped hard boiled eggs, apple cubes, chopped pickles, capers, chopped chives, celery salt and mayonnaise. Dill and parsley optional. Let marinate 1 hour. Serve cold.

II. Cut Fleischwurst or baloney in strips each about 1 inch long. Mix with chopped boiled eggs, chopped pickles and mayonnaise. Optional: Capers, dill, chives. Decorate with boiled egg slices or wedges, dill, paprika, caviar, green olives, pimentoes, tomatoes or a combination thereof. Let marinate 1 hour. Serve cold.

HERINGSSALAT (Herring Salad)

6 pickled herring
3/4 lb. cold roast veal or beef
2 apples
1-2 large cooked red beets
1 large cooked potato
1 medium onion
2 rounded tablespoons crushed walnuts
3 large sour pickles
2 tablespoons vinegar
2 tablespoons water
mayonnaise

Remove heads, tails and bones from herring. Peel apple, potato, beets, and onion. Dice all ingredients. Add mayonnaise, vinegar and water. Mix together well. Let marinate in refrigerator 6 hours or overnight. Decorate with egg wedges and parsley.

FREIBURG
LOCAL COSTUMES

M. NELSON

Soßen

Sauces and Herb Butters

Sauces make the difference between the master cook and the can warmer.

The herb butters add the final piquant touch to a well prepared meal.

HELLE GRUNDSOSSE (Basic Cream Sauce)

2 level tablespoons butter or margarine
4 level tablespoons flour
1 pint soup stock
salt
pepper

Melt butter. Stir in flour and brown very lightly, stirring constantly. Add soup stock slowly, stirring with an egg whisk to prevent lumps. Cover. Simmer very slowly, stirring occasionally for 10 minutes. Salt and pepper to taste. Serve hot with meat, vegetables, fish, and fowl.

HELLE GRUNDSOSSE FÜR GEMÜSE (Basic Cream Sauce for Vegetables)

Prepare as for Helle Grundsosse, but substitute the water in which the vegetable was cooked for the soup stock. Add vegetable before serving.

DILLSOSSE (Dill Sauce)

Prepare Helle Grundsosse, after cooking is completed add 1 heaping table-spoon finely chopped dill. Cover. Let sit for five minutes. Do not cook. Serve hot with boiled fish and boiled eggs.

KAPERNSOSSE (Caper Sauce)

Prepare Helle Grundsosse. Add 1 to 2 heaping tablespoons capers with the soup stock. After cooking, season with lemon juice. Remove from stove. Beat 1 egg yolk. Add 4 tablespoons of the sauce to the beaten egg yolk and stir in. Add egg yolk and sauce mixture to the sauce slowly while stirring. Do not cook. Serve hot with meats, fish, fowl, vegetables, potatoes, and eggs.

HOLLÄNDISCHE SOSSE (Hollandaise Sauce)

There are several "quicky" recipes for Hollandaise sauce, but they just don't make the grade. Being a lover of Hollandaise sauce I made this recipe generous. If you are going to this much trouble let's have enough of it.

1/4 level cup sifted flour
1/4 cup cold water
4 eggs
1 pint soup stock, strained and clear
2 tablespoons lemon juice
1/4 lb. butter
salt

Mix flour and water together well. No lumps. Combine flour and water mixture, eggs, soup stock, and lemon juice together in the top of a double boiler. Beat together well with an egg whisk. Cut cold butter in chunks about as big as beans.

Put top part of double boiler over boiling water. Whip constantly. While whipping add the butter chunks one at a time until they are mixed in.

Continue cooking, whipping constantly until mixture thickens. Salt to taste and serve immediately. Incidentally, some people add either one teaspoon of hot German mustard or 1/2 teaspoon of grated nutmeg to Hollandaise sauce, but I don't recommend it.

Serve with broccoli, cauliflower, Schwarzwurzeln, Brussels sprouts, asparagus, fish, fowl, and veal.

PETERSILIENSOSSE (Parsley Sauce)

Prepare Helle Grundsosse. After cooking, add 1/4 cup finely chopped parsley. Cover, let sit five minutes. Serve hot with fish, potatoes, vegetables or eggs.

SARDELLENSOSSE (Anchovy Sauce)

Use either 3 ounces of anchovy fillets in oil, drained, or 3 ounces of salted anchovy fillets that have been soaked overnight in water. Finely mince anchovies. Add to Helle Grundsosse with soup stock. Add 1 tablespoon capers, optional. Season with lemon juice.

Serve hot with meats, eggs, fish, vegetables, and potatoes.

CHAMPIGNONSOSSE (Mushroom Sauce)

Clean mushrooms or use drained canned mushrooms. Slice mushrooms in thin slices and brown them in butter. Prepare Helle Grundsosse. Add mushrooms with soup stock. Season with lemon juice.

Serve hot with meat, vegetables, fowl, game, potatoes, and eggs.

ZWIEBELSOSSE (Onion Sauce)

Prepare Helle Grundsosse. While adding flour add 2 finely chopped medium onions. Add 1 rounded teaspoon caraway seeds, optional. If a slightly sour sauce is desired add 1/4 teaspoon sugar and 1 to 2 teaspoons vinegar.
Serve hot with potatoes, vegetables and fish.

SENFSOSSE (Mustard Sauce)

Prepare Helle Grundsosse. Add 2 rounded tablespoons of mustard after sauce has cooked 5 minutes.
Serve hot with meat, fish, eggs, and potatoes.

KÄSESOSSE (Cheese Sauce)

Prepare Helle Grundsosse. Add 1/4 to 1/2 lb. finely grated cheese after sauce has cooked 5 minutes.
Serve hot with meats, vegetables, potatoes, and noodles.

WINDMILL IN THE
LOWER RHINE COUNTRY

GEWÜRZBUTTER (Seasoned Butter)

Slowly melt 1/2 lb. butter in a sauce pan. Do not stir and don't let it cook. Skim off and discard the foam that rises to surface. Remove from heat. Add 1 teaspoon lemon juice, 1 teaspoon Worcestershire sauce and 1/2 teaspoon ground mustard. Stir in. Let sit 1/2 hour. Rewarm, do not let cook. Salt to taste. Sprinkle with 1 tablespoon freshly chopped chives or parsley and serve immediately.

Serve hot on fish.

PETERSILBUTTER (Parsley Butter)

Slowly melt 1/2 lb. butter in a sauce pan. Do not stir. Do not let cook. Skim off and discard the foam that rises to surface. Add 1/4 cup finely chopped parsley and salt to taste immediately before serving.

Serve hot on fish or boiled potatoes.

KRÄUTERBUTTER (Herb Butter)

1/4 lb. butter
2 level tablespoons finely chopped fresh parsley
1/2 rounded teaspoon ground dried tarragon
1/2 rounded teaspoon dried dill
1 rounded teaspoon finely minced fresh chives
1 rounded teaspoon dried chervil
1 rounded teaspoon minced onion
2 teaspoons lemon juice
salt

Allow 1/4 lb. butter to come to room temperature. Whip with a fork until light and fluffy in a small steel or glass saucepan. Important -- not aluminum. Add all ingredients and whip together. Let stand overnight in a cool place. Salt to taste. Whip lightly just before serving.

Serve well chilled on hot fried, baked or roasted meats.

SARDELLENBUTTER (Anchovy Butter)

Allow 1/4 lb. butter to come to room temperature. Whip with a fork until light and fluffy in a small steel or glass saucepan. Important, not aluminum. Finely mince 4 one-ounce cans of anchovy fillets in oil, drained, or use 4 ounces of anchovy paste. Whip together. Let stand 2 hours.

Serve chilled on crackers as snacks or use as garnish on meats, game or fish.

SENFBUTTER (Mustard Butter)

Allow 1/4 lb. butter to come to room temperature. Mix 2 crushed hard-boiled egg yolks, 1 level teaspoon ground mustard, two tablespoons lemon juice, salt and pepper with the butter in a steel or glass saucepan. Important -- not aluminum. Let stand 2 hours.

Serve chilled on meats, fish, fowl, or vegetables.

HEIDELBERG

Gebäck

From the oven

APFELSTRUDEL

These will be some of the best calories you ever put in your mouth. There is enough here to serve six Bavarians or six Americans.

For the pastry:
3 level cups sifted flour
2 level tablespoons sugar
1/8 teaspoon salt
2 eggs
3 tablespoons ice water
1/8 lb. butter

For the filling:
3 lbs. juicy apples
1 cup sugar
1 cup raisins
1/2 level tablespoon cinnamon

158

1 teaspoon rum

For decoration:
1 egg yolk
2 teaspoons sugar
1/2 cup slivered almonds

Measurements are important here. Sift the flour once, then lift carefully into a measuring cup with a spoon. Heap slightly, do not pack down or tap cup, and cut off with a knife or spatula. Add the sugar and salt and mix together. Add the eggs and mix together. Add the ice water a tablespoon at a time and knead together. Knead the dough well 5 to 10 minutes. The dough will be very stiff. Form into a ball and set aside, covered, for 1/2 hour.

Peel and core the apples. Cut in very thin slices, about 1/16 inch thick, lengthwise, not rings.

Take one half the dough and roll out as thin as possible in a rectangle on a lightly floured pastry board. Pick up the sheet of dough. Make fists of both hands, drape the dough over your hands and pull your hands to the outside. This stretches the dough. Be careful not to tear. Continue this until the sheet is very thin, always working from the middle toward the edges, about 18 inches by 14 inches. This sounds harder than it is. It's really quite easy. Lay the sheet of dough on a well floured pastry cloth. Melt the butter and paint the sheet of dough with 1/2 the butter.

Take 1/2 the apple slices, mix with 1/2 cup sugar, 1/2 cup raisins, 1/4 level tablespoon cinnamon and 1/2 teaspoon rum. Spread immediately on the dough. Roll together tightly to form a long roll. Tuck in the ends and press together to seal.

Repeat the above to make the second Strudel.

Butter the oven tray (at least 18" long and 12" wide with raised sides) well and preheat the oven to 475°. Beat the egg yolk and paint the two Strudels with egg yolk. Sprinkle a teaspoon of sugar over each and 1/4 cup slivered almonds over each. Bake as follows: 10 minutes at 475°, then turn heat down to 400°, and bake 20 minutes, then turn heat down to 300°, and bake 15 minutes. This "stair-stepping" of temperatures is very important.

Remove from oven. Remove Strudels from pan and set on a large serving tray. Pour the juice from the pan over the Strudel and set aside to cool. Serve either hot or cold. I prefer it ice cold.

OBSTTORTE

A Torte is half way between a pie and a cake. Now is when we run into problems. You see you don't have the proper pans in the States to make these. So I will give the recipe as it is made in Germany and add a variation so you can make it in America.

2 egg whites
2 tablespoons cold water
2/3 cup sugar
1/4 teaspoon vanilla extract
1 cup sifted flour
1/2 level teaspoon baking powder
2 egg yolks
butter
1/3 cup fine bread crumbs

For the filling:

Canned or fresh fruits. (If you invite ME to dinner I love fresh strawberries and bananas.)

1-1/4 cups fruit juice from the canned fruits, if fresh fruits are used, use 1-1/4 cups water.

1 rounded tablespoons sugar, if fresh fruits are used use 3 rounded tablespoons sugar

1 level tablespoon cornstarch

For decorating:
whipped cream
toasted, slivered almonds

Rub a 12 inch pie pan with butter, pour in bread crumbs so it is completely coated. Beat the egg whites and the cold water to stiff peaks. Beat in sugar and vanilla. Fold in beaten egg yolks. Sieve and simultaneously fold in flour and baking powder. Spoon batter into pan, smooth out and bake in a preheated 375° oven 10 to 15 minutes. Remove, turn out of pan and let cool.

The German Obstkuchenform has a depression about 3/4 inch wide and 1/2 inch deep running around its outer edge so that after the Torte is turned over you have a nice little raised edge so you can put in the filling without it running out over the kitchen floor. But since you don't have this, we are going to have to make some improvisations. Prepare a firm vanilla icing, put it in a pastry tube and build a nice little dam, like the one on Lake Nasworthy, around the edge. This should be about one half inch high. Now we're ready for the filling.

Arrange the fruits on the Torte. It should be practically covered. Stir the water or fruit juice into the cornstarch slowly and stir well so that there will be no lumps.

When all is mixed together well (incidentally, you can use some food coloring here if you wish) bring to a boil, in a small pot, stirring constantly. Cook 1 to 2 minutes, stirring constantly, until the mixture clears, then pour immediately over the fruits on the Torte. Make sure all fruits are covered. Set aside to cool. Decorate with whipped cream, grated toasted almonds, and serve chilled.

ORIGINAL MÜNCHENER BIERKUCHEN (Loaf Beercake)

In the introduction I said that coffee was not just coffee, but coffee and cake. To quote Frau Bleininger: "The cake (Bierkuchen) tastes best to wine or coffee."

1-3/4 cups sifted flour
1/8 lb. butter
2/3 cups sugar
1/3 cup dunkles Bier (dark beer)
1 egg
1/2 level teaspoon baking powder
1/2 teaspoon powdered cinnamon
1/2 teaspoon cloves, whole
1 cup large white raisins
2 ozs. candied citron peel, finely diced
2 ozs. candied orange peel, finely diced
1 tablespoon rum

To decorate:
1 jar apricot jam
roasted pistachio nuts or roasted almonds

Crumble the flour, butter and sugar together between your hands in a mixing bowl. This should have the consistency of coarse sand. Stir in all the other ingredients. Butter well a loaf pan, 2" deep, 4-1/2" wide and 13" long, and sprinkle with flour so that the pan is completely coated. Heat oven to 350°. Pour batter in pan and bake until done, about 1 hour. Turn Kuchen out while still hot and spread with jam. Decorate with a stripe of pistachios down the middle. This can be eaten warm or cold. I prefer it cold the next day.

BESIDE
SELENTER LAKE

zu Hause

Family dishes

Recipes to serve four

After the big meal at lunch time and coffee and cake in the afternoon most Germans eat a light dinner in the evening. These are the dishes you will find for the evening meal in a typical German household.

ABGEBRÄUNTER LEBERKÄSE MIT SPIEGELEI

No true Leberkäse exists in the U.S. unless you find a German butcher. As a poor substitute use luncheon meat or a slice of baloney 3/4 inch thick.

Brown Leberkäse well on both sides. Top with a fried egg. Sprinkle with chopped chives. Serve with hot or cold potato salad and a good cold beer.

AUFSCHNITTPLATTE (Cold Cut Platter)

Set out a big plate of assorted cold cuts, a package or two of Camembert Cheese, a few slices of assorted cheese, a can of sardines, cold potato salad, tomato wedges and chopped chives for decoration, with butter and black bread.

BISMARCKHERING MIT PELLKARTOFFELN (Herring and new potatoes)

Serve canned pickled herring cold, garnished with onion rings and boiled new potatoes, hot, with parsley butter.

EIER IN SENFSOSSE (Eggs in Mustard Sauce)

8 eggs
Senfsosse — Mustard sauce, see pg. 155
mashed potatoes
pimentoes

Boil eggs. Remove shells. Place a generous helping of hot mashed potatoes on each plate. Stand two eggs small end up in the mashed potatoes and pour mustard sauce over eggs. Garnish with pimentoes. Serve with a mixed or green salad.

ERBSENSUPPE MIT WIENERWÜRSTCHEN (Pea Soup with Wienerwursts)

1 package of dried yellow pea soup mix
   or
2 cans yellow pea soup
4 strips bacon
1 rounded tablespoon flour
1 rounded tablespoon lard or shortening

1/2 small onion
salt
pepper
paprika or chives

Cut bacon in 1/4 inch lengths crosswise. Peel and dice onion. Melt lard in a pan and fry bacon and onions until onions are glassy. Stir in flour. Add soup mix or canned soup according to instructions on label. Stir well to prevent lumps. Simmer slowly for 10 minutes. Add wienerwursts cut in 1/4 inch lengths. Simmer an additional 10 minutes. Salt and pepper to taste. Garnish with paprika or chopped chives. Serve with rolls or black bread and salad.

GEBACKENE LEBER (Fried Liver)

4 slices of tender calf's liver
lard or shortening
2 large onions
2 apples
salt
pepper

Peel onions and slice in thin rings. Peel, core, and s ice apples about 1/4 inch thick.

In a large frying pan melt lard and fry liver and onions together. Add apples about 5 minutes before liver is done, otherwise they will overcook. Salt just before serving. Serve with boiled or mashed potatoes and green salad.

SALZKARTOFFELN UND CAMEMBERT

Boiled potatoes, butter and Camembert cheese is an evening meal favorite.
Wash and boil potatoes. Peel. Serve hot with plenty of butter, salt and pepper, cold Camembert cheese and black bread.

SCHWEIZER WURSTSALAT (Swiss Wurst Salad)

Slice Lyoner, in America, baloney, into thin slices. Slice Emmentaler, Swiss or Cheddar cheese in thin slices. Cut slices in 1/2 inch squares. Slice an onion in thin rings. Mix together. Add salad oil, vinegar, salt, and pepper. Marinate 1 hour.
Serve cold, garnished with finely chopped chives or parsley and egg wedges.
On separate plates serve thickly sliced black bread and a mixed or green salad.

REIBEDATSCHI (Potato Pancakes)

Make potato pancakes, see pg. 120. Serve hot with apple sauce and/or cranberry sauce and a green salad.

SPINAT MIT SPIEGELEI (Spinach with Eggs, sunny side up)

8 eggs
enough chopped frozen spinach for a generous serving for four persons
1/4 lb. butter, no substitute
1/4 level teaspoon ground nutmeg
butter for frying eggs, no substitute
salt & pepper

Prepare spinach per directions on package using as little water as possible. Mix in butter and nutmeg. Simmer an additional 5 minutes. Top with fried eggs sunny side up. Serve with Salzkartoffeln, pg. 121, and black bread.

GEFÜLLTE PFANNKUCHEN (Filled Pancakes)

1 lb. flour
2 eggs
1 quart milk
lard or shortening
salt
filling, see opposite page

Make a pancake batter of the flour, eggs, milk and salt. Wipe a hot griddle with a paper towel and a little lard. Make pancakes about 8 inches in diameter. While still hot, add about 2 tablespoons of any of the following fillings and roll together. Place in the oven to keep warm until serving.

Suggested fillings:

scrambled eggs with or without catsup
chopped boiled eggs in Senfsosse, pg. 151
diced fried ham
diced leftover meat with or without catsup
fried tomatoes
asparagus with or without white sauce
cauliflower with or without white sauce or Hollandaise
fried or creamed mushrooms

LACHSBRÖTCHEN (Salmon Sandwiches)

Slice rolls in half. Make open face sandwiches, with sliced smoked salmon. Garnish with onion rings, capers and mayonnaise.

INDEX

books designed with giving in mind

Pies & Cakes
Yogurt
The Ground Beef Cookbook
Cocktails & Hors d'Oeuvres
Salads & Casseroles
Kid's Party Book
Pressure Cooking
Food Processor Cookbook
Peanuts & Popcorn
Kid's Pets Book
Make It Ahead
   French Cooking
Soups & Stews
Crepes & Omelets

Microwave Cooking
Vegetable Cookbook
Kid's Arts and Crafts
Bread Baking
The Crockery Pot Cookbook
Kid's Garden Book
Classic Greek Cooking
Low Carbohydrate Cookbook
Kid's Cookbook
Italian
Cheese Guide & Cookbook
Miller's German
Quiche & Souffle
To My Daughter, With Love

Natural Foods
Chinese Vegetarian
The Jewish Cookbook
Working Couples
Mexican
Sunday Breakfast
Fisherman's Wharf Cookbook
Charcoal Cookbook
Ice Cream Cookbook
Blender Cookbook
The Wok, a Chinese Cookbook
Japanese Country
Fondue Cookbook

from nitty gritty productions

THANKS

To: Frau Bleininger, a very charming lady, for the recipe for Original Münchener Bierkuchen; Frau Brüggemann, whose tortes are extraordinary, for dutifully tasting so many spices to help me identify them and for advice on spicing; Herr Brüggemann, a gourmet, who loyally served as official guinea-pig as we tested recipes; Eddy, my girl Friday; Maya Gebhard, a very good cook, for the recipe for Sauerfleisch; Emmy Hammerer, the best cook I know, for so many good German meals; Bob Kesterson, an engineer who likes egg plant, for many helpful suggestions in the text and format; and to Ruth Kesterson, the type of American that leaves a good impression in a foreign country, for testing recipes.

For the pages that follow I wish you a "Guten Appetit".

F. Miller
Munich

NEUSCHWANSTEIN CASTLE
NEAR SCHWANGAU

M. NELSON